It's Impossible to Commit to Maybe

A BOLD GUIDE FOR
BUSINESS MANAGERS

David R. Lumley

PAGE PUBLISHING
Conneaut Lake, PA

First originally published by Page Publishing 2022

ISBN 978-1-6624-5810-1 (pbk)
ISBN 978-1-6624-5812-5 (hc)
ISBN 978-1-6624-5811-8 (digital)

Printed in the United States of America

CONTENTS

CATEGORIES

A. Getting Started
   Chapters 1, 2, 3, 4, 5, 6, 7, 8, 9

B. Managing: The How and Why of It All
   Chapters 10, 11, 12, 13, 14, 15, 16, 17, 18, 19, 20, 21, 22, 23, 24, 25, 26, 27

C. Management Challenges and Solutions
   Chapters 28, 29, 30, 31, 32, 33, 34, 35, 36, 37, 38, 39, 40, 41, 42, 43, 44, 45, 46, 47, 48, 49, 50

D. The Management Politics Game
   Chapters 51, 52, 53, 54, 55, 56, 57, 58, 59, 60, 61, 62, 63, 64, 65, 66, 67, 68, 69

E. The New Frontier
   Chapters 70, 71, 72

F. Learnings
   Chapter 73

G. Beyond Maybe—Some Book Two Topics!

H. The Spouse's/Mom's Perspective on Chapter 52: But We Are Afraid of Jackie
   Chapter 52A

INTRODUCTION

This book is dedicated to my dad. He passed away in 2014 at eighty-two. It was he who told me, "It's impossible to commit to maybe." It's on that simple but powerful platform this book of business, family, friends, foes, and life learnings is all about!

Its sole purpose is to give you and others some things to think about…and then act upon!

I have used analogies in stories throughout my life to try to communicate both difficult as well as humorous messages! That approach usually worked, although at times, some people thought the stories or comments were too straightforward. In the end, we are all adults, regardless of business experience, race, creed, wealth, or nationality, and we should hopefully treat everyone the same—as adults. I have always tried to do that.

But let's get to it. This book has a lot of chapters because those headings are subject statements about a particular learning. I hope they are a good guide to help you quickly see what you'd like to explore. This book contains my learnings and opinions. It is meant to be useful and enjoyed. It is also designed to help you look at issues you are facing in business—or even your personal life—and get a different perspective (to help you move forward!). In no instance do I think I am a psychiatrist, philosopher, a unique business leader, a great parent or boss. These stories are simply here for you to take a look at, and if they help you in any way, that's great. There are also five categories the chapters are loosely organized in. Again, just a guide.

So why is this book named *It's Impossible to Commit to Maybe*? It's a great story, and I will "tell it" later in detail. Quickly though, it's something my father told me after a golf round when I asked his advice regarding the fantastic lady I've been married to for over thirty years now. But it also crystallizes the very messages in this book. I hope they help you in some way, and remember, have some fun along the way. It's a one-way trip!

Thanks to Becky Stilwell, whose tireless typing, editing and spellchecking made this book possible. To Tommy Lumley whose graphics work provide the book's cover and a lot more. To Veronica Genito for her absolute blast of honesty in chapter 52A and great guidance. To everyone who provided all those opportunities and learnings at Western Illinois University. Finally, to all those who have helped along the way to help me to commit to success and help others do the same.

GETTING STARTED

CHAPTER 1

"Stay in Formation, Follow the Plan"

That seems a simple enough statement...a simple enough strategy. In my entire career, however, I have found it's one of the single most difficult things for people in a business to do. This is especially true in situations where the board and/or the owners are more involved than normal.

Still, in today's world, we have activist shareholders in public companies who buy 1–10 percent or more of stock and become operations experts overnight, believing they can run the company better than the management team. (Rarely, however, do such people want the responsibility of operations results...) Certainly nothing wrong with someone who invests their money to have their opinion. However, the board hired a CEO and a management team to run things, and at times, it takes a commitment of time to "stay in formation, follow the plan" until you are successful.

I learned about the approach (stay in formation, follow the plan) from US military history and the movie *Twelve O'Clock High*. Some of you may have even had leadership courses based on this film. It is based on the true story of a US Air Force strategy in WWII to move their bombing raids in Europe from night to day. They were having trouble hitting their targets at night and had a lot of casualties. Planes would also leave formation to go help those in trouble as they flew in on their bombing runs. What they found was, the more planes that went after those in trouble, the more they weakened the group. The more they stayed in formation, the stronger they were and the better chance they had of getting there and back and hitting their targets…ones they could see in the daylight. That was the plan. Those who did not follow the plan were put in the "leper colony" and lost their command. Many people I have worked with over the years will tell you they too were put into the "leper colony," whether it was a business or region or spending approach, when they didn't stay in formation!

If you "stay in formation and follow the plan," you can have tremendous success. Here's a great example: Any time you face a difficult company or business turnaround situation, it is actually then you have the greatest opportunity to fix it. The closer you are to failure or even Chapter 11 in some cases, the faster you decide. What is the biggest problem in any plan? Indecision. Playing it safe. Not taking any chances. Or just do what they said in MBA school—spend, spend, spend and somehow it will get better. We know those things don't usually work. Develop your plan. Stay in formation. Get everyone on board. Go. Execute, execute, execute. Come back, reward those who do it. Those who don't, who go out of formation, get them off your team…to the "leper colony!"

There are numerous examples I have been involved in about the importance of following the plan. They include a nutrition company with family ownership sold to a venture capital group, a controlled public company that actually did come out of Chapter 11, a large division of a very well-known large consumer company that was left for dead, and a bicycle company where the odds against it were so high that one would have to be able to compete with products that cost as much to make as the new retail price of the competition's products.

Let's talk about the privately held nutrition company (with the young founder, family, and friends still involved). The "old plan" (which worked until a few years before the sale) was to just sell the products via direct (mail) and specialty stores. The "new plan" was to sell to the mass market as well. First challenge? No one knew how to do that!

So we brought in some new people, taught the existing team several new tricks, and developed the new plan (sub-brands for mass, three channel products/pricing, great new targeted advertising, leveraged and benefited greatly from the founder's book and fitness challenge).

"Staying in formation" here meant believing in the new products and distribution channels. Following the plan meant executing it without falling back into the "old way."

Here's the rub: People don't tell you the (whole) truth. They are more afraid of failing than trying to win…and they really only want to do what they know how to do (which is fine if you want your company to have to be sold again!).

So how did we get everyone to "follow the plan"? We separated the distribution channel groups but paid everyone on the total numbers. Sure, there were some individual targets and payouts, but "Compensation and Organization" (more about that later) drive behavior…period. (Don't believe me? Armies march and win with food in their stomachs and gold in their pockets…)

Then there is change, success…the plan starts working. It's consistent leadership, a lot of communication, and relentless *execution*.

The results? The company more than doubled in size, grew EBITDA four times, and sold to one of the big boys.

Got it? Want another story? How about a large consumer goods company that wanted so bad to be twice its size it bought companies too fast, for too much money (overpaid), and grew its debt to equal its sales (you read that right). As you would expect, it's much easier to buy companies than to integrate and operate them successfully.

It became a '60s conglomerate forty years too late. Now perhaps everyone thought it "was a good idea at the time." (Wall Street did at the time, buying into the $5B vision size). The challenge quickly became the debt service, slow to achieve synergies and brands that were good but not number one in any category. The MBA model (I do have one of those, but I just don't think a whole company of such educated people, especially with inferior brands and a lot of debt, is a good recipe for success) pushed the team to go (out of formation), spend a lot of advertising dollars to establish the brands, hire only folks from big companies (who were used to big brand budgets), and create a matrix organization at odds with itself—everywhere. No formation; individual plans…which equaled the old plan.

When things went bad, they tried to sell certain divisions (too late), and Chapter 11 arrived (which is actually even more costly… and brings out all the piranhas…lots of them).

What to do? Step 1, get out of Chapter 11!

How? *Stop doing what put you in that situation*. Sounds simple? Not so. Remember the Nutrition Company story? Just like there and the mass market, no one knew how to do that, and no one knew how to get out of Chapter 11 here…or so they thought.

Step 2: Take stock.

What do you (really) have? What are you good at? What are the competition's strengths/weaknesses? Are you really important, *in any way*, to your trade customers and/or consumers? Are there market gaps? Needs?

Get rid of your ego. (You are, by the way, in Chapter 11; the bonuses, stock, severances, everything…are *gone*). When you "have to" do things, no matter how difficult or risky, you "can." If you "do," you will move fast and make more "right" decisions than any other time in your career.

We got into formation and developed a plan. Then we executed it for years and years. It worked, really worked, but it took a lot of "staying in formation, following the plan." Even our principal owners wanted to break formation at times, especially early on. *But* we had one or two real believers, whom we partnered with (plenty of rough skies, but it worked). That company grew to over $5 billion, the *promise* the previous board/team *promised* but not via their ever-changing plan.

How did it happen? How can you do that? We believed our brands could be the best price/performance products in our channels; we challenged the competitor brands with claims and better prices. We provided more margin to our customers (and beat their private labels…even if we had to do the private label first). We won in the stores (and invested all the brand consumer advertising spending into in-store promotions.) We built the most efficient supply chain in the business with 3–5 percent cost improvement *every year*. Then we stuck to it. Very few liked it at first. It was and is hard work. The results? Five straight years of premium bonuses. Stock grew five times the post Chapter 11 issue price. Market cap soared to over $5 billion. Success. (Impossible, you say, without consumer advertising? Not for us. Number Two's can win a lot of ways but not by out-advertising giant number one brands. We proved it. You can too.)

There are several other stories and companies. We can visit those later. The strategy was always the same.

Stay in formation. Follow the plan.

CHAPTER 2

Stormy Seas Make the Mariner

My first turn as a president, I reported to a former nuclear submarine commander who was the chairman and CEO where I worked. He had tremendous presence, was very smart, and had a great track record. He had given me a second chance when I had a showdown and lost with my former company CEO over some very big issues that, granted, later turned out that I was correct about but, at the time, taught me an important lesson. Being right or having the board members encouraging you to take bold action is great, but if you don't get it in writing, it is not going to happen. (Chapter 39) But that's not the point of this chapter. The point of this chapter is two of my new CEO's lessons: "Great mariners are not made in calm seas" and "Do what you say, when you say."

We all want to be successful. To do that, we have to achieve positive results. That usually means taking some risks, accepting a difficult assignment, perhaps moving outside or within the company and/or geographically.

Here I left one marine company for another. Because of legal restrictions, I had to work in a non-marine business—in this case, bicycles. The CEO had led a diversification strategy and acquired several sporting goods companies. One segment of these acquisitions was a leading mass market bicycle brand and a number seven independent bike dealer (IBD) brand known for BMX (kids) bikes.

The bicycle companies were smart buys at the time until the US government dropped tariffs on Chinese-made bicycles and brands.

This dramatically changed the US market. Approximately thirteen million units per year were sold in the United States in the late nineties, the majority US-made. Bang! Chinese bikes soon were priced at retail at the manufactured *cost* of US bikes, including the two brands the CEO asked me to take on. It presented numerous challenges:

1. The CEO wanted his acquisitions and strategy to be a success.
2. Chinese bikes had a *huge* advantage in price (and were well-made, with plenty of features).
3. Retailers quickly converted to imports on an alarming rate since few at the time had a well-known IBD brand.

Calm seas quickly turned very stormy for me and my CEO. What to do? What did we have (left)? How could we win?

Following many of the learnings presented in this book, we (the bike team) took a good look at what we had (US plants, two brands, one an IBD brand, a CEO who supported us, and a possible compensation plan that would reward risk-taking).

We reduced our SKUs (lowering costs), relentlessly reduced cash (a trip to Taiwan/China to see our competitor taught us a lot—they didn't even provide toilet paper or other essentials for workers), capitalized on the world's largest merchant's need to have bicycles (a very seasonal business) on a timely basis (used US plants and built a Mexico plant for our two largest mass models, enabling us to supply in weeks versus the months it took from China), utilized our small IBD brand to go "cross-channel" to the mass market (putting us first as an IBD brand vs non-branded imports), and got a special compensation plan approved for our team. "In formation, following this plan," we became the number one unit brand in the United States.

We did what we said we could do when we said we could. Our CEO got the board to pay the unusual compensation plan. Our all-for-one organization and compensation plan worked. The "stormy seas" subsided. We all became true mariners.

The lesson here is, difficult challenges make you better. They prepare you for future "storms." Learn. Your team needs true mariners. Always.

CHAPTER 3

It's Impossible to Commit to Maybe

We will see how it goes. Time will tell. If you do this, we might do that. Let's test it, try it out. Get the picture?

What you're really saying is maybe. Maybe you'll move your family. Maybe you will eventually get married.

The lesson here is a hard one.

How does anyone commit to "maybe"? Two examples—one personal, the next business.

Personally, I had been dating my now spouse of thirty-plus years for quite some time. Lots of reasons we had not gotten engaged. Quite a personal story. Still, the fact was it had been too long, especially since I did not want to lose her. Finally, she said to me, "I love you, and I will miss you." That was it. Gone. No meetings, phone calls, letters, or any response to my communication attempts. Three weeks and counting. My world was in chaos.

I had a golf outing planned with my dad. So off we went. I tried numerous times to explain to him what was going on with my girlfriend, but he was focused on golf. No real input from the sage!

After golf, in the parking lot, I pressed him one last time. His response floored me. It became one of the fundamental approaches to my business and personal life. He calmly, and in less than sixty seconds, laid it out.

1. "You love this girl?" (Yes.)
2. "You don't want to lose her?" (No.)

3. "But it appears you have?" (Hopefully not!)
4. "Well, you are asking her to commit to you only on your terms..." (Yes.)
5. "But you aren't committed to her?" (Well...)

"So you know, Dave, it's impossible to commit to maybe." (Maybe someday we'll get married.) "That is what you are asking her to do."

That was it. Boom!

It's absolutely the same in business. Commitment is a two-way street.

- You guys fix the company. *Maybe* we will pay you this.
- California-based VP wants the promotion, but *maybe* he'll move his family to the new location per requirement.
- We go into the board together to present a controversial plan, but if it gets challenged, *maybe* you can count on everyone on the team to stay together?
- Tell Sales if they hit the number, *maybe* you'll pay the double commission you outlined.
- If your best customer wants A-B-C, *maybe* they will give you more business.

You get the picture? You don't want to commit to maybe. Why would you ask others to?

You see, it's impossible! So do the right thing—commit to the task, the move, the team, the company or move on. You want to be counted on all the time, not just when it's good for you or them.

You see, I believe "Do what you say, when you say you will do it." It works! (She married me!)

No maybes.

CHAPTER 4

Hope Is Not a Strategy

Developing and executing a winning strategy is challenging. Strategy, in its most basic form, is a plan comprised of all or several of these elements: research, competitive analysis, product/service positioning, manufacturing, sales, marketing, pricing, creativity, and financial support/goals among other areas. Strategy can be conservative, bold, based on past successes, something new, or a combination of the aforementioned or more.

A winning strategy requires thought, testing if possible, line organization buy-in and commitment, support by ownership, and outstanding execution.

A great strategy with poor execution usually fails. An average strategy with great execution can still work. A strategic plan is usually based on an idea, a concept, or a path; it can be clever or obvious.

Your strategy may be born out of a company process, need, envy, desire, luck, or financial requirements. It may be for the well-being of others. It may be just for your well-being!

To achieve a successful strategy, it will ideally be simple to understand, execute, and fund. The telling sign you don't have a winning strategy is when you "hope" it works! You "hope" others will understand it. You "hope" management will support you.

Turn all that silent hope into a new action plan. Go develop a winning strategy based on facts, input, creativity, customer needs, and your strengths. Here are some examples:

1. *Home and garden division business.* We competed with three other large companies. The leaders had bagged goods (fertilizer, mulch, seed) and chemicals (weed killer). The second had both categories as well but was more price-oriented. The third was a division of a large corporation and focused only on chemicals (roach, wasp, ant, etc.). Our division, purchased a few years before I arrived, was trying to provide all products and categories. Our product performance was good, but the now new division lacked well-known brands, had a smaller on-site merchandising field force than the leader, and struggled with the bagged goods business. The existing strategy was lower price versus the leader, key private labels for the big three customers, and consumer advertising (but much less than competitors). This was a seasonal business and vulnerable to COGS raw materials increases for its bagged goods.

   The "strategy" was to "hope" something would succeed among all the products. Remember, this hope, however, didn't have the brands, merchandising, advertising, or insulation from COGS increases (that they could pass along to the customers).

   The division did have well-performing products, especially in chemicals. These were also manufactured in the United States at their own plants. In addition, due to the nature of these products, they were very difficult to develop and get approved by the USDA. Chemical products were also the most profitable.

   Still, the corporation and division were convinced without both categories, bagged goods and chemicals, they would fail completely. The "hope" strategy and fear now combined to cause this business's EBITDA to fall by 50 percent when COGS increases hit. Customers, especially on their private labels, still would not take much in price increases or try to pass on those price increases at retail. Hope turned to big losses.

The division became frozen in place. With no success with pricing, the next step was to "hope" we could sell the division. It was tried and, in the end, failed as well. (Strategic buyers had their own problems.)

Here's where a real strategy was born. It was finally a necessity at this point and still very difficult for the "hope team" to embrace.

We have covered how to develop and roll out a strategy (see Chapter 31). Here we did just that. The strategy, based on our strengths (chemicals, good performing products), was developed and launched. First, we exited bagged goods. We then passed the bagged goods store brands back to the stores (free but with requirement, they continued to buy chemicals). We transitioned bagged goods facilities to retailers/new suppliers. Then we would become the best (only) home-and-garden chemical company. We positioned our well-performing products as "same performance, less price" (than the leader). We dropped the focus on private labels. The result was less sales, but EBITDA soared back to previous levels and beyond. Hope was replaced by a real strategy that won and still works.

2. *Personal appliance promotion.* Strategy is involved in just about everything in business, not just at the corporate or division levels. We owned a leading personal care company. We were strong in men's and women's electric shavers and women's hair dryers, styling irons, and so on.

We had a $10 million promotion order opportunity for women's products at a key retailer. Our team, pressed for time, quickly put together a price promotion, same product and packaging as in store, and presented it. They actually said they "hoped" it would win. It did not. In fact, the retailer, so underwhelmed, threatened to replace those product's placements for everyday distribution as well

($30 million more!). Once again, hope was not a winning strategy.

We then developed a real strategy for promotions. We received intelligence that key purchasers of hairdryers and styling irons at this time of year were driven by high school-aged women. Our staff, who had just provided little strategy here except price, was comprised of all women. We encouraged them to do research, look again at the competitors' products and prices, and develop a strategy to appeal to the target audience—high school women. They conducted several consumer focus group sessions with young women. Our staff, who were all ten to fifteen years older than the focus group participants, were told they "didn't understand" by our focus groups. The focus group women told us they liked to get together to use these products before events. The new strategy was then born to determine how to appeal to the young women when they got ready together for the prom and/or spring break and other events. They said they wanted a good product that was graphically "cool" (to show their friends), same with the packaging, and at a decent price!

The young women who were in the focus groups actually did some designs and graphics for the packaging, colors, and promo names on the boxes. We embraced our strategy of user input and took the new products back to our customer and won the promotion and expanded our everyday listings.

So after hope was lost, a new creative strategy (ask your users!) won. Big or small, a winning strategy is right there waiting, while others keep hoping things magically work out.

A hope and a prayer is really something. In business, however, a good strategy makes those prayers come true!

CHAPTER 5

It's a Long Race

It's your career. "Live long and prosper," says the Vulcan (*Star Trek*). Just how long are most business careers? About thirty-five to forty-five years! That's right, and it's never too late to have a plan, to learn, change, advance, and succeed.

When I first graduated with my master's degree from a big school with my new job starting the day after graduating, I was pumped.

Your first job, as you probably remember, was a shock. Up early, work long hours, and then do it again. Pay wasn't as good as you thought, and why were there so many people who made more money (and didn't seem to do much) than you?

How about those friends of yours who barely graduated now selling (something like insurance) and making more money than you?

Well, that happens…at first. Careers take many different paths. Timing, personal decisions, opportunities, and your drive all impact your path and end result.

It's never too late until you truly check out. Did you or do you have a career plan? Why not?

I know people who plan their vacations better than their career! In fact, in all the management development training we did, this was the number one issue and opportunity. A plan. Let's get this race started and review your situation:

1. What was your college major? (Ha ha, I know.) Why?
2. Are you still interested in that area? Why? Why not?

3. How did you (really) get to your present position? Are you happy? Is it part of a bigger plan?
4. Is money your principal driver? If not, what is?
5. Are there personal considerations holding you back? Can they be altered?

Add up all these answers, and you will see where and why you are where you are.

Now,

1. What do you want to do?
2. What do you have to do to get started in developing your plan?
3. Write your plan out. Consult with your life team. (See Chapter 61.)
4. Revise, adapt, and get comfortable with your plan. It's got to be your plan; no one else is going to do it for you.
5. Start to execute your plan. It will take time, patience, drive, commitment, and changes to your personal life. It will work if you stay in the race.

I had a poster in college; it said, "I don't know where I am going, but I am on my way."

That's pretty close to where most people are. A better poster says, "You can't get to where you are going if you don't know where you are going."

Personally, I wanted to be a journalist when I was young. All through high school and college, I actually made money doing just that. Northwestern's Medill School of Journalism was my goal for grad school. It happened. My career plan was to be the next Mike Royko (famous *Chicago Daily News* columnist).

Everything was going great until I found out starting journalists didn't make enough money to pay off student loans!

My plan changed to PR and advertising! Then to marketing, then to sales. Then back to MBA school (while I worked—very challenging). Then into general management. Several companies. Then CEO, with financial success in my fifties.

The plan, however, stayed true from my thirties on: Get to the CEO chair. I put in the time, personal sacrifices, work, and commitment the plan required. If you learn, listen to your life team, and stay on course with your plan; it will work.

It's a long race. You can win it, regardless of where you start, as long as you have a plan and follow it through.

Go!

CHAPTER 6

Go with Your Strengths

The number one question I got from graduating college students, interns, and young managers when I was CEO was...when should they get their MBA degree?

My response was always the same: "Why do you (want) feel you need an MBA?"

Their answers are summarized here:

1. Because they had been told top managers have (needed) an MBA to be successful.
2. They wanted to expand their business education.
3. It would help them make more money.

All those responses can come true. My experiences, however, tell a different story.

The most effective managers I have worked for, with, or who reported to me were successful based on being in a job where their personal strengths were in play most of the time. The great salespeople were really good at selling. The CFOs matched their strengths in accounting, finance, and managing expectations to their job and its key audiences. The operations leaders were really good at math, systems, and tracking things. All of them were strong in the key areas required in their jobs. Few, if any, had MBAs.

It doesn't mean there are no situations, jobs, and life plans that don't benefit from the time and investment required to get an MBA; there are. (I was one but not until I was thirty-nine years old!)

Still, for most managers, going with your strengths, being committed to your life plan, and focusing on achieving good results will usually get you to your goals faster (and with less debt!). Now going with your strengths is a lot more involved than getting an MBA or not. Your strengths (and passion) can be applied to several career paths, industries, companies, and jobs. Following your instincts are key here. Going with your passion, interests, and strengths usually works! Following the herd, most likely, will not be as successful for you.

Yes, expanding your knowledge, education, experiences, and geographical posts are all good for your career—but more college, travel, and nice-to-knows rarely play key roles in the building blocks of a successful career.

Relentless focus, effort, persistence, and using your talents, skills, and drive elevate your career. Use *your* strengths. A sports analogy comes to mind: You may think being the fastest runner on the team is the ticket to stardom. The thing is, what if you are not a very fast runner? You can practice technique, run sprints, lose weight, gain muscle, and work out every day. You still may not be fast or the fastest runner. You are, however, say, very strong. It's a "strength" (pun intended!) of yours. It matters. Play the position where it's important. Go with it. Dominate. Use your strength(s) to succeed. That's why you have them.

Here's an example.

There was a promising operations manager at my last company. He believed he needed an MBA and should be stationed only in the corporate office and get experience running sales and marketing as well so he could become a CEO someday. Understandable. He felt addressing his weaknesses would solidify his quest to reach the top. You see, though, when you abandon your strengths to primarily focus on your weaknesses, it leaves you, well, weak at your job. (I realize these are generalizations and a very black/white view; still, business is unforgiving.)

Now he was competing with much stronger sales and marketing managers at our company and, more importantly, versus our competition. This was a big personal care and small appliances business. His strengths in sourcing, purchasing, and overall operations were being overshadowed by his lack of experience and strengths in sales and marketing.

He lost shares and sales while he tried to learn. The operations side suffered as well. Ultimately, he lost his job.

Perhaps, if he would have stayed with his strengths, he could have surrounded himself with people good at his weaknesses. Learned from them. Learned on his personal time. Supplemented as needed.

The "strength" approach worked very well for myself and many I worked with in my career. Ask yourself, What are you best at? Why? Are you using your strengths? Why not? Determine this and consider a life team (see Chapter 61) review. The choice, of course, is yours.

It's your career. My learnings point to a strength-first strategy. Getting stronger in all areas takes time. A strong base is a good place to start and rely on. Ask yourself, What kind of managers do you want on your team, the strong ones or those working on their weaknesses?

CHAPTER 7

Chaos Is an Opportunity

Frequently, I have been asked how I became a CEO.

There were several steps (see Chapter 31), but a key conscious decision I made was to embrace chaotic situations and companies in chaos. If I saw there was, despite the risks, a good opportunity there due to that very chaos, I would run toward it rather than away.

Several great companies with very capable people run on all cylinders. Rarely is there much chaos or change. That also means many managers wait a long time to learn, move up, or experience real challenges.

Those of you who would rather be tested early and often, build on your plan (see Chapter 5), develop yourselves, and seek out chaos.

For example, go work for the company, division, department, or job that's in crisis, in need of a turnaround. You say you don't know how to do that. This is how you learn. You will be much better for it and move more rapidly through your career. (See Chapter 2, "Stormy Seas")

In each case I did this, I got stronger, more confident, and more able to do it on a grander scale. The next time this meant job satisfaction, income, rank, and flexibility. It's the difference between "How did they do that?" and doing it. It also can lead to the top of your game.

Sure things, no chaos, and safe and steady jobs are fine if that's what you want. Successful leaders, however, are usually crafted in battle.

Chaos is unsettling, challenging, and at the same time, scary as hell.

It also might be the biggest opportunity you may ever get.

CHAPTER 8

Anticipation (or Work the Worst Case Backward)

Everything is gonna come up roses!

We are going to grow the company, the stock price will zoom up, and everyone is going to be rich!

Huge promises without a real plan, one that doesn't try to "anticipate" the challenges ahead, usually end up in a worse position than where the company started the "new plan." Why?

Anticipation is a critical skill and process most leaders bypass too often in their rush to implement and work "their" plan. The problem is, the competition, your customers, consumers, suppliers, and world governments have their own plans. Sometimes these plans, actions, and needs change the playing field and drastically affect your plans. Some examples: bankruptcies, acquisitions, tariffs, rising interest rates, unemployment, strikes, new products and services, R&D breakthroughs, new technology, leadership changes, wars, etc.

Spend time to study and anticipate such possible changes by revisiting your company plans, your key product lines, segments, suppliers, customers, consumers, competitors, energy availability and costs, and local financial and government policies and ask, "What is the worst-case scenario?"

You say that's too theoretical! Really? Let's look at some things that happened in my career:

- Oil went from $10 to $40 to $150 a barrel in a very short time.
- Tariffs on some goods tripled or were eliminated.
- New technology replaced entire businesses.
- Our key competitor could make its product for 20 percent less than us.
- A key customer dropped our biggest line.
- Key plants' unions went on strike.
- We (almost) lost our key license to brand the bulk of our sales.
- Our key supplier failed.

Most companies' risk analyses are around their IT system. That's appropriate. Still, think through your business, your supply chain, key customers and employees, key government and economic policies, etc.

Anticipate challenges ahead of time. It's a daily job. Once something bad hits without a plan for it, it is too late. Top athletes, business leaders, governments, and moms and dads all have this skill. It's learned, not given. You can develop it. Practice it. Make it a daily consideration.

What will they do? What will you do if this or that actually happens? Is it about to happen? (George Washington won the US Revolutionary War principally because he used spies to "anticipate" the next moves of the British.)

Anticipation. It makes your "speed model" faster. It also keeps the ship afloat in storms.

Try it. What do you anticipate could happen tomorrow? Next month? Next year?

Money Losers Rarely Get Better

Every company, division, department, product line, product, brand, office, customer, supplier, investment, consultant, ad program, plan, employee hire, and just about anything else that has a cost at a company has one thing in common—the sponsor.

It's that employee or group of employees (including the board members and investors) who decided an investment was warranted. Let's call these sponsors or persons the parent(s). Like most parents, they want their children (investments in this case) to succeed. They also don't want to ever admit those children are misbehaving or failing (like losing money).

My experiences taught me it's these sponsors (parents!) who continue to "hope" their investments (children!) will succeed. So rather than dealing with the issue on an objective business level, they find numerous ways to hide the problems, make excuses, and delay the inevitable—cutting the investment off.

You may say, "But this book has numerous examples of turning things around that were failing." That's true…except it's the scope and breadth of failure we are reviewing here. In most cases, companies get in trouble due to poor leadership. Here, we are addressing the need to deal with obvious consistent money losers. (See Chapter 11)

It can be in any area outlined earlier. Usually, however, it's certain products, brands, customers, and international sales regions.

These "money losers" are relatively easy to get started, usually in response to the competition and/or trying to rapidly expand sales.

The problem is that with such "hopes" (see Chapter 4), these investments are not well thought out. These losers can also be long-time neglected products or regions as well. In either case, the results are the same—consistent money losers, distracting the company from better investments, and depleting precious resources.

A regular sales and margin review of all SKUs (stock keeping units), customers, and sales regions P&L yield the true facts. It's here the resistance builds within your organization. Not only are the sponsors blocking the elimination of the money losers but usually sales and operations as well. (What will replace the sales? The volume through the plants?) So maybe you need the money losers? That's how ridiculous these arguments get.

Everyone's job is to build winning investments. If some fail, okay, then eliminate them now. You say some things take time. Okay, was that outlined in the launch plan? Was it accounted for in the P&Ls? Doubtful.

Business is pretty straightforward. Things work or don't. Some investments are great to okay. Many are not even okay. They are the money losers and my learnings in almost every case; they rarely get better on their own. Trim the tree, we learn, and it grows better. Same with investments. Trim…if no growth, cut it down. Move on. Examples aplenty!

1. Sales Region—Latin America

    At most US companies I was at, we had global sales organizations. Usually, these units were divided into regions. In this case, let's talk about the Latin America (South and Central America) region at my last company. Here, we sold numerous consumer products. In one country, Venezuela, we used to do well. In the last three years, however, things continued to decline. The reasons were clear: political and economic upheaval and currency declines. Still, our international sales leader was from Venezuela. He had friends there. He worked very hard to try to save the business. Still (he was the sponsor or parent!), we lost money each year on his "child"!

It took another year, even after all the attempts to make the country profitable, to finally close it down (the office, direct employees, and warehouse). Why so long? For all the reasons outlined previously—denial, hope, emotion, hiding the worst, and finally, stubbornness. Significant losses. We needed to exit earlier but kept trying. The extra cost? Over $15 million more in losses (profits, currency, bad debt, government issues). Money losers rarely get better...but they can get worse!

2. Specialty Customer

Same company but in the United States, we had a large customer, not a big box but good volume and distribution. The problem—not only was it not very profitable but they also started to employ questionable business policies. These included unauthorized deductions for returns, quality, co-op advertising and volume. They also stretched invoice payment terms to two to three months past due dates. This pushed the account profitability to zero or, at times, negative. (You'd be surprised how many companies don't regularly look at total customer P&Ls.) The account became and stayed a money loser for two more years (always with promises and plans to the contrary from the account and our sales teams). Sponsors! What to do?

We developed a new plan for the account, rewarding both them and ourselves. They agreed. We lost more money. What? You see, they were failing as a retailer and trying to survive off the deductions, discounts, rebates, and sales without paying for the goods for long periods.

Again, the sponsors (parents) fought hard within our organization to stay the course. Like in our Latin America example, facts (actions) are needed to be considered first. Finally, the CEO had to make the decision. We exited the account. They went Chapter 11 (bankrupt) the next year. Money losers rarely get better—some go bankrupt!

Now these same situations, facts, and actions are everywhere in your organization. Brands, products, promo programs, etc. Here's a simple approach to change the tide:

1. Evaluate the money loser objectively.
2. Get all the facts.
3. Review with all appropriate audiences.
4. Develop plan to make money—quickly.
5. Execute plan.
    a. Works? Great.
    b. Doesn't work? Exit the loser.

Money losers rarely get better on their own. You can fix that!

MANAGING: THE HOW AND WHY OF IT ALL

Everybody's in Sales

You know, many people go to college to get a business degree and/or later an MBA, and many think they want to be a GM, the top boss. It's always stunned me, however, how *sales* seems to be a dirty word in this quest. Just think about that. Without sales, there is no company, no CFO, no CEO, no board. Without sales, there is no supply chain; there is no brand.

Sales is the lifeblood of a company. I believe everyone is in sales: customer service, marketing, finance, purchasing, HR, and R&D. Some of the most successful sales calls I have ever been on were when we took the head of R&D or a product specialist or someone with knowledge and credibility who could answer the customer's questions or could give them a different perspective. Team selling is a proven approach. Almost no one does it. At times, many salespeople show up for presales call dinner, walk the boss around, and play politics. What a waste of time. I also found that one on ones before or after between the top person at the trade customer and myself were much more effective. The truth comes out. You talk about the real issues. No boss knows everything that's going on. Large group meetings are a bigger waste of time.

As you go into your business career, go out to the field to visit the plants and suppliers as much as you can, talk to your customers, and meet the buyer and the buyer's boss. Talk to your salespeople, listen, go to lunch/dinner, and spend some time with them. Ask them what they think. What are their frustrations? I always wanted to know who the best salespeople were…and usually, they were the ones that the home office people have the most problems with, as in "Boy, if we just didn't have these salespeople, our life would be good." It's almost as bad as if we just didn't have customers—just think how easy our job would be! Great salespeople *push* your organization. They make you better and make your company more money. They are your "army."

When you talk and listen to your best salespeople, you usually find a common thread: They drive, they ask for things, and they over-forecast—they do all those things because for the most part, your company's systems are inefficient. The company is slow. People in the home office—whether they are in purchasing or marketing or R&D—rarely actually go to see the customer or go to the plant. Do your people know if the third-party plant can make the new product up to the specs the home office has developed? Has anyone asked the customer or consumer? We always made our marketing people go to the big accounts, help prepare for the line reviews, and go on those calls. It's easy to sit in the home office and say that customer doesn't know what they are talking about—we are smarter—if you have never been there, in front of the customer.

You know there's a great saying in a book I read about the military. The general said he learned more in the twenty minutes he was on the ground, on the battlefield with the troops, than he did in two hours or two days flying over the battlefield.

Same idea with sales. As the leader, you need the same credibility the general does on that battlefield. Actual field experience. Learn sales. Do it. Then find great salespeople; interview them yourself.

Then work with all departments to make sure sales has products with "a real reason to buy!"

Passion, energy, drive, ego, reward, recognition. This is what makes a great salesperson. It doesn't mean that everyone has to be a dynamo. It simply means "prepare." A lot of people can sell a product everyone wants. It's hard to sell a product when you actually have to sell it on its real merits, its "reason to buy."

"Reason to buy?" Seems easy to understand. Few products get there. Is it the price? Is it the brand? Is it the benefits?

The RTB is elusive, as most consumers don't entirely know or won't admit why they like a particular product. So ask them again and again. Look at POS at several trade customers. Usually, a consumer buys a particular product because they "understand" its benefits. Someone has explained the RTB. Online. Chatroom. Friends. Advertising. PR. Packaging. So figure it out and then communicate it! "Fastest Acting," "Best Taste," "Best Performance," and of course, "Best Price/Performance!"

When you want to sell a buyer something, you also need to understand what the buyer(s) thinks and how the buyer is compensated. A great boss I had once told me, "Organization and compensation drive behavior." I will talk a lot more about that in another chapter. But if you don't know how the buyer whom you are trying to sell is compensated, you most likely aren't going to do too well (and you won't be in sales very long!)

Once you understand how the buyer is compensated, you need to think like they have to think. They are trying to grow the category, not just your product. And they have to present and sell it to their boss. And remember, all buyers in that store or that Internet site are vying for the same checkout locations, front of the store, best part of the store, the promotions, what's on the Internet and what's not. See, you are not only competing with your direct competitors; you are competing with what everything your buyer has to sell versus other things in that department, that store. You need to know and develop a plan that works in that environment.

So if you understand those things, you can pitch promotions and locations and where to put your products as part of a total program to help your buyer—your trade customer—to succeed. Also, buyers care a lot more about what's in the ads of their competitors than what your consumer ads are or what your competitors' consumer ads are. For instance, in morning meetings when their boss comes in and says his boss asked him why the store they are competing with has a better ad price than they do on your product, you both have a problem! (Anticipate!)

So when you are doing a line review or a category review, you need to also present how your products will fit in versus the other stores they compete with, and if you are really smart about it, you will have slightly different products and slightly different price points so that they fit together. Think about your two hands—the fingers should intersect between your two hands just like the products and pricing between the two or three big retailers competing. Yes, that requires more work by your category team. Yes, that requires more work by your marketing team. That's why it's called team selling and that's how you win. (Everyone in formation!)

So you want to be the "boss"? Spend time in sales (directly if possible), and never stop being a salesperson. You will be much better at your GM job, earn the respect of your organization, and help push your organization to greater success. Everyone is in sales…including you!

CHAPTER 11

80/20 Always Works

You might have learned about this in school, were told to look into this, or might have been told to do this analysis approach. It's really a finance or operations thing, you may think, not really for you. Simply put, in my view, it's one of the keys to fixing most companies.

So what is this miracle analysis again?

Your product lineup (stock keeping units or SKUs) drives tremendous activity in your company. Every SKU has escalating costs as it ripples through development, marketing, sales, operations, IT, finance, accounting, customer service, D&T, and customer returns.

The more SKUs, the more cost…and inventory, storage, support services. Every SKU has a parent (sales, marketing, R&D, customers, consumers) and never wants to leave the party!

The 80/20 analysis approach isn't new, revolutionary, or difficult to understand. What is very difficult is to do it and then act on it. It's a gold mine. It's also almost impossible to successfully mine that gold without the total commitment of the CEO and everyone in the supply chain. So what is it? Your team launches a review of every SKU for their sales and margin. Group the top SKUs that produce 80 percent of the margin, and then sales. Cross reference these two lists as well. There are your best products. All the rest are costing you…a lot.

Now drive out what will be close to 70–80 percent of your total SKUs out of the company.

Yes, do it. You can since their total margin and/or sales creates massive costs and activities with little return.

To do this, you will need weekly meetings for at least a year, especially with sales and marketing. Develop substitution plans for certain products, then go meet with customers and reach agreements.

Finance, IT, and operations will love this. Everyone else will die on their swords to save all "their" products. Doomsday predictions. Customer revolts!

You see most of these products lose money, especially with a total cost accounting review. They use and tie up a lot of cash (slow-moving inventory) and warehouse space. They are holding the company hostage.

So once you get these SKUs in order, do a commonality of parts/ingredients analysis. This will lower COGS costs and increase margins. For instance, at my last company, we had hundreds of fish food SKUs, containers, and ingredients. We reduced SKUs 50 percent, ingredients 60 percent, and increased common ingredients in more than 40 percent of SKUs. We relaunched. Millions of dollars of savings. Sales went up since they were now in stock and delivered on time.

In the marine business, we found we had over 1,400 outboard motor SKUs. That's right. Just fifteen platforms but so many custom offerings. There were numerous colors, brands, different parts, propellers, etc. On and on.

Guess how many of the 1,400-plus SKUs produced 80 percent of the sales? About 125. How about 80 percent of our margin? About 40.

We pivoted the brands, colors, and specialty builds. Again, deliveries, service rates, and sales went up (after year one). Savings? Eight million dollars.

Why do you think Southwest Airlines routinely has the best, on-time service and usually makes the most money? They have only one jet (737), all similar parts at the airport, and everyone knows how to service the jet. Fly the jet. This all means speed. Reliability. Lower costs.

How about In/Out Burger? Really successful restaurant chain. No chicken sandwiches, no pizza, tacos, or specialty drinks. Just burgers, fries, and drinks. Commonality of ingredients. SKUs focused on the 80/20, in their case, 90/10.

You say that's great, but your company is too complex for this. Sales will decline; customers will flee!

Nope. Every company will benefit from this approach. In every case, when I arrived at one of the seven companies I worked at, each one had this issue. The companies in the most trouble were doing the worst. Too many SKUs was their top issue and opportunity. Can't grow sales? Do 80/20. Want to improve service? Do 80/20.

For instance, a very well-known plastic storage company had 112 types and colors of plastic storage bins. Yes, that's right. Each retailer had their own line!

The losses were in the multimillions due to rising oil prices (plastic was 60 percent of COGS), no retail price increases, and this SKU nightmare. Remember, every SKU requires R&D, IT, finance, accounting, operations, sales, marketing, and customer service to touch it, track it, make it, store it, ship it, and update it…on and on.

We took the 80/20 approach to the furthest degree. We turned the company around. Massive savings everywhere. Turned out all the consumers could be happy with just clear, gray, black, and white containers. That's four, not over a hundred! We also turned R&D into a cost *savings* department!

At my last job, a conglomerate of consumer brands I led, we got 3 percent cost improvement (of COGS) almost every year with this approach (versus 0–1 percent most companies achieve). Margins went up. We streamlined marketing and sales, D&T, IT, and operations. Less complexity. Less wasted activity. Better service and sell through. Remember, as my great-grandfather (a grocery store owner) said, "You don't get a second chance to sell that product that's not on the shelf." Get your product out on time!

Still not a believer? In the seven companies I led, we achieved record numbers in CI, margin improvement, and through put. It worked every place and every time. It's easy to develop and launch products and advertising. The 80/20 is what pays the bills.

It is hard work. All the time.

Want to fix things? Save things? Want to reach 100–200 percent bonuses every year?

80/20. No more excuses. No "hope" advertising programs. Dig in. Do it.

80/20 works 100 percent of the time.

CHAPTER 12

One More Time?

What are "they" doing (your previous company)?

You retired or left. It felt good. You adjusted. It's better than working...or is it?

The company you retired or left from doesn't seem to be doing as well or at least what you think they should be doing or achieving.

Sound familiar?

Maybe they will ask you back? Maybe they should?

Do you want to go back? Why? Really?

It's probably normal to have those feelings.

If you don't, that's great! If you do, then what?

Perhaps you left too soon? Or didn't like "how" you left? Or maybe you don't like who's running things now.

You do usually have choices. Some of them are obvious; others not so much.

1. Get over it and get on with your life!
2. Try something new.
3. Join a board.
4. Become an advisor.
5. Start (something).
6. Buy (something).
7. Have more—spend some of your money!
8. Read.
9. Volunteer.

Notice there's nothing on the list that says, "Go back to where you retired or left from."

Famed author Thomas Wolfe wrote *You Can't Go Home Again* (a book about such actions). It's a very thick book. Maybe you should read it!

Yes, a few entrepreneurs have taken back their sold companies and made some money, but that's the exception. Some very good pro athletes have tried it. Usually doesn't work out so well.

Going back with your old flame rarely worked, so why should this? You left for a reason because you must have wanted to leave. It most likely won't be better this time either.

Go forward. Revitalize yourself in the business world like you have in your personal life since retiring/leaving. Go now. Go forth. Go a different path. This is a gift. Cross the Rubicon. Back is the wrong way. It's simple. You graduated. You got your grades. Use them for something better!

CHAPTER 13

Plan B

A famous boxer once said, "Everyone has a plan until I hit them in the face and they go down, then they need a new plan!"

Plan B. Do you have one for your strategy, department, company, or career? Not really, right?

That's what I thought. Most people don't. We are a species that tends to wait until things force the issue. The problem is by that time, it's too late (to avoid real problems).

Our enthusiasm, our ego, and our limited time to develop such plans usually leave us without the "what if" or "What do we do if it doesn't work out?"

It's similar to making sure you have an escape route in threatening conditions—fire alarms and escapes, life preservers, smoke alarms, 911, even car horns!

So why do the majority of companies and their divisions, departments, and campaigns rarely have well-developed Plan Bs? Do we think that it is not showing confidence in Plan A? The new strategy? The new hire? Probably. Still, it's why a seasoned boater never leaves port without a full fuel tank and an extra five-gallon container. I hear airline companies now shorten fuel loads to save/make more money. Appears smart, eco-friendly, and faster. It also could mean a very deadly and explosive crash. Happens all the time in day-to-day business. Plan A will be great! No Plan B. Crash!

Most of my career, I was the "turnaround leader," the fixer. Not a popular job. You see, it's a lot more fun to develop Plan As, spend lots of money, and conquer the world! Who needs Plan B?

More times than not, Plan As with no Plan B means leaders like myself are Plan B. You are no longer in charge. Everyone quickly shifts to the "blame game." It's universal. And you will pay the price.

You want examples? Too many to list! Let's just say my last five president jobs were all based on Plan A failures by the former president/CEO. Now there are other reasons besides no Plan B for failures, but a good Plan B and even C most likely would have kept the ship from sinking!

So who should develop Plan B. You…and a few other experienced team members.

When do you develop Plan B? Before you approve and launch Plan A.

Be prepared. It's your responsibility. It's your future. It's so much better than a turnaround guy like me showing up in your office!

CHAPTER 14

Natural Leaders

Who and what is a natural leader? The CEO? President? The best sports player? A father? A mother? A politician? Are leaders born? Can you learn to be a good leader? Perhaps all the above but none of the aforementioned are necessarily a "natural" leader.

These natural leaders can be a hidden key to success in any endeavor. It's your job to find them, listen to them, and realize they are as important as all the high-titled executives on your team in getting things understood and moving.

A natural leader usually has the pulse and the ear of your employees. They get things done. People listen and follow them.

So you ask, "Who are these people and how do I find them?" They are right in front of you. They are the person at the shipping desk that when things really need to get done, you are told to just deal with her/him.

When things are not working well, you find they have been trying and trying to get management to listen to why and how it can be fixed.

They are respected because they "know"; they have been there, done that. They have worked for a lot of bosses for quite a long time.

It's not about titles, income, race, creed, politics, education, or personality. It's about who people trust, respect, and will respond to all the time, not just when threatened.

First thing I did when I joined a company was to go out and find and listen to these natural leaders. What you need to know is there. Save the money on consultants.

You may think it's too time-consuming. Your staff should know those things. Well, the information won't get to you. Too many management layers. Too much politics. Too much everything. If you get to them, it will actually save time and money and reduce inefficiency.

How do you do this? Visit the docks, plants, and department meetings. Hold a breakfast/lunch roundtable. No bosses allowed! Your town hall.

You will see the natural leaders instantly. They will speak up with passion. As one famous military general said, "You learn more on the battlefield in two hours than you do two days flying over it." You can also ask those you learn to trust around you who the leaders are. Then seek out those natural leaders they tell you about. Listen, understand, communicate, tell their stories, and watch your department and/or company fly!

CHAPTER 15

The Real Offsite

Let's plan a strategy meeting in a real cool place. Plan fun "team building" activities and suddenly get creative!

Then the meeting attendee list grows and grows as it becomes a political, career-messaging event. Costs go up and up. The company's productivity drops. Those not invited freeze, worried or curious about what it means. What is going to happen? All this sound familiar?

You say, "Wait…offsite strategy meetings are needed. They can be successful. Great team-building opportunity." So are drinks at the local bar after work, I hear.

The real offsite is different. It is a small group. Little cost. Close by to headquarters or easy to get to. You have a simple goal: how to be better tomorrow.

Develop a short, simple agenda. I found four or five people is ideal. Best is the financial leader (CFO or like) and division heads. Same goes if a department or division meeting. Try to get a moderator so the boss (you) isn't leading the meeting. You want the truth to come out and gain meaningful ideas. Why have the meeting otherwise? Have the moderator talk to each attendee before the meeting. Get grounded on key issues, challenges, and needs. Publish that list, one to two pages maximum.

Go somewhere comfortable. We did such meetings on a small boat at a ski resort in the summer, at a golf club, or at a rented cabin.

No big dinners or events. Regular food and drink brought in or bought at the store. If you want some exercise, then do that as a team.

Talk openly, no politics! Get it up on the flipchart for all to see. Have the moderator lead discussions and take notes. Stay on task. No going into "all the other issues."

Some titles (or themes?) of off-sites I participated in (and worked!):

- Who are we, the company, really? Knowing that, how do we win?
- How do we cut $50M out?
- What is our vision for the company?
- How do we organize to position the company to succeed?
- What is our exit strategy?

You may say those singular topics are not enough. They will be. Pick the "burning issue" at your company. Everything will fall into place from there. Two days will do it. Prepare. Talk. Listen. Revisit. Decide. Go.

You can then go on a great personal vacation to a cool place and have fun after your off-site strategy is working!

CHAPTER 16

Supply Chain Is the Key

Speed kills…your competition. Think Walmart. Uber. Military victories. Sports stars. McDonalds.

First product developed. First shipped. First delivered. In stock…always (Frito Lay!). It's called the supply chain. Not sexy like marketing, advertising, or even sales. It's a long string of actions and people with lots of challenges, roadblocks, speed bumps, and bottlenecks.

It requires the most planning and coordination in the company. It is also one of the absolute keys to long term company success.

A solid infrastructure with a resulting great supply chain will make your company competitive with anyone and a preferred supplier to your customers/consumers.

So how do you build, fix, improve, and/or utilize such a weapon? Some basic data I always started was the following:

1. What are your company's fill rates? 100 percent? 95 percent? Less?
2. What is your product cycle time from raw materials delivery/order to receipt to customers? Weeks? Months? Same for purchased goods.
3. What are distribution times? Start to finish?
4. What are your competition's numbers? (Ask your customers!)
5. Are your suppliers' partners (meaning they offer cost savings and faster cycle times) or just lowest bidders?

6. What are your quality control returns (percentage by key supplier)?

7. Are you faster or slower than last year? Year before?

8. How much business are you losing by being late? Out of stock?

9. Is your forecasting system effective? What is its accuracy? (Are you forecasting based on actual shipments or order requests? Your actual forecasting number is the shipments versus orders requested.)

10. What do your supply chain people say?
    - How can the company do better?
    - Are there too many products?
    - Remember the 80/20 SKU discussion? (See chapter 11) Too many SKUs bog down any supply chain.
    - Do you know what the total cost of an order to fill is? Break small orders versus large orders as well. (We reduced shipping costs for ourselves and the largest big box store by simply understanding this and changing the deliver strategy from direct to stores to regional centers.)

Lots of questions, I know. It doesn't matter how good the product is; it's marketing or sales or advertising. If your supply chain is inefficient, slow, and can't meet demand, you will fail.

Know that a lot of things impact the supply chain. Map out the entire chain, especially in problem areas. Find every step, every bottleneck. Fix them. Civil War Union General US Grant won key battles, he said, in part based on his supply chain approach (constant supplies in time). Speed is everything. Speed is a direct result of your supply chain.

Winning companies do a lot of things right. Supply chain is usually at the top.

I would offer that companies who invest in their supply chain excel at it and usually win. The rest play catch up…at a huge cost.

CHAPTER 17

Attack Their Strength

David versus Goliath. Good story. It provides hope in battles of the big versus the small. The strong versus the weak. Problem is, hope is not a strategy.

In the real business world, you need a plan, one that can provide you time to find answers to your challenges. In the case of competitive battles, say P&G products versus your number three alkaline battery brand, you need an edge, a reason to buy versus your competition.

In this case, the leading brand was the "most trusted," backed by a lot of advertising and the broad distribution strength and rebate programs of the P&G company.

So exactly what was that leading brand's key strength (they had several!)?

One of their key strengths was their distribution program, backed by P&G tie-in rebate programs and incentives, "impulse" consumer buy checkout locations in stores, and payments/pricing to keep number three brands out of the stores.

In addition, these batteries sold well but provided less margin to the retailers. We could not out-advertise them or out-"incentivize" them or, most of the time, even get distribution in "their" stores.

So we "attacked their strength," that being they were perceived to be the "most trusted" battery based on how long the batteries lasted. We found we could manufacture our batteries in the United States to last as long as their batteries, provide better pricing and margin to the retailers, and dare them to respond to our claim, "Lasts as long, costs less."

By attacking their strength, we got distribution based on their weakness-retailer margin.

It worked and kept working until my team left the company.

Yes, conventional wisdom is to attack your competitor's weakness, which we did…but only after changing the selling proposition by attacking a strength they could not afford to change without admitting we lasted as long as the number one brand but cost less.

You can do it too. Figure it out. Be bold. Get stronger!

CHAPTER 18

SG&A Is Not an Entitlement

Selling, general, and administrative (SG&A) expenses. It is the first place you can look when joining, studying, or trying to determine what is going on at a company, division, or even a department is the SG&A line on the financial statement.

Why? Because usually these expenses are too high, allowing inefficiencies to exist, hiding mistakes, and showing too much staffing, pay rates, and just lots of overspending.

It also is where yearly employee salary raises are, many times, regardless of employee performance. How about medical plans? Pension plans? 401K costs? Training? It can go on, depending on the size of the business—selling, rent, advertising, marketing, accounting, litigation, travel, meals, bonuses, and more.

So what is a good SG&A percentage of sales? Rates?

Each industry, geographical location, and in what political/tax environment the company operates in will yield different ranges and averages.

Once you understand these ratios, it will be easier to improve in this area.

Study the trends in the industry and your company. The goal? Reduce SG&A. Keep it tight. It's a lot easier to do a 10 percent reduction in force or cut bonuses or advertising as an event rather than a process. Find out what is really driving your SG&A. Usually it's too many people. Extra people really exponentially increase SG&A costs, usually at an alarming rate.

On top of these costs, companies usually provide across-the-board salary increases. Yes, union contracts require yearly wage increases but not administrative or management employees.

SG&A increases, ideally, need to be earned with demonstrated employee performance, advertising that increases sales/sell-through, and travel costs that produce measurable results.

Unfortunately, SG&A tends to increase yearly based on perceived entitlements, not demonstrated results, that then produce more requests for more spending.

A great way to improve productivity in all areas of SG&A is pay (only) for performance, as in positive results. Eliminate and/or reduce SG&A otherwise at every turn.

A very effective method we used was zero-based budgeting. (Do you still need so many finance or IT personel? Three layers of management? All that advertising? Do you need to travel with three people to most sales calls?)

The result was leaner, more effective organizations with everyone contributing, with only necessary staffing and spending.

Entitlements are very expensive, usually with no guarantee of better performance or results.

Dig in and challenge all these costs. You will have a big push back from your poor performers and/or the overspending groups but a much-welcomed response from those you want to keep, the ones driving the company!

So did it work at the last three companies I was part of? Never missed a bonus. Achieved one of, if not the best, SG&A rates in our industries. We routinely reduced SG&A rates every year.

All that led to increased market share, sales, and financial results.

You see, performance pays…best.

CHAPTER 19

You Are Always Recruiting

Hire a recruiter. Get HR on it. Post the open jobs on the web. That's how most companies recruit. It's the accepted way to fill open and new positions. Is it effective? Sorta. Are there better ways? Of course!

One way to build a better company is to find the best people you can for the jobs needed to succeed. To do that, everyone, especially those who will be this person's supervisor, must get and stay involved. Getting the right person is very important, yet so many managers believe it's HR's job and they are too busy to also work hard to help find that person. This is the norm—even though each manager's department and/or team will directly benefit by the right hire. It is not enough to get the job approved for hire. That's just the beginning. One usually doesn't get engaged or married without participating in the pursuit or process!

I always spent a lot of time on the lookout for great talent at any level. Friends, references, those at meetings, competitors, customers, family referrals (be careful here!), trade shows, suppliers, interns, college alumni, you name it.

So you want to build great teams? Then recruit all the time. Never stop. It's your job, one that will pay very big dividends.

Remember the Russian doll. (See Chapter 28.)

Go buy one. Put it on your desk. It will remind you every day how you can help make your team better and bigger!

CHAPTER 20

Barbells

A metal bar, weights, and at each end...barbells.

As I was taught by one of my mentors, that's what a company is like. The weights at opposite ends being the people who make it and the people who sell it. Everyone else is the bar that supports those weights.

It's the very essence of an enterprise. No products made/sourced, no company. No sales, no money, also no company. Without either, no need for anyone else.

Now usually, when I rolled out this philosophy and importance of building our companies this way, almost everyone responded as you would think—their department was really the key area. Finance (money providers, they said!), Marketing (really in love with themselves!), R&D (the creators!), HR and Legal (sorta agreed!), Service (sided with the makers), and Senior Management (kings and queens always believe they are the most important).

The learning here is simple: The people and organizations that make and sell your products are the only ones directly tied to the customer process and success. They know what is needed, when, where, how, at what price, who can help make it, ship it, deliver it, and fix it. Only they know whom you compete with directly on the front line and what suppliers and customers say, want, and need.

A strong barbell doesn't bend or break or slip. It supports the makers and sellers. Every person. Every department. It keeps things in perspective. Otherwise, self-centered leaders and departments can rise up, take over, and shift focus and funds away from the makers/sellers to their political needs, spending, investments, staffing, and strategies.

Time and again, this happens, and it results in decline in company performance—first in product costs and delivery rates, then market share losses, then great salespeople leaving and finally overspending in (the bar) support areas.

You say that we need to be a marketing-driven company or to improve our financial management or to change our culture. Fine. Do that. Support groups need to be the best they can be. They don't need to artificially direct the company or use funds better invested in making and selling. It shouldn't ever change the barbell and the weights approach. Strengthen that bar. It then can hold up bigger and better weights, allowing the company to make more and sell more and produce more money…every day.

Remember, when you lift more weight, you get stronger.

Give Your Company a Call

How well does it go when you call (any) company? Customer Service? Maybe a customer? A supplier? A consultant? Are you happy with the response time? Did the call meet your expectations? Would you recommend the company/person(s) you called to others? Not that often?

Why? Computer or robot voices? Long hold times? Your calls go direct to voicemail? If not a service issue, can you reach someone in person who can help you a challenge? How does that make you feel about that company? Probably not so good!

Now think about your company—from sales to customer service to your personal number. How well do you think your company is doing with people who contact the company? Do you know what your customer service wait times are? How well are their responses and solutions received? What are your quality issues? Delivery times? Top billing questions? Finally, do you know the number of times (on average) it takes others to reach you? If not, why not?

So let's try calling your company...right now. Call customer service or the returns department. Call billing. Call your number.

How long did it take to reach someone? Did they treat you well? Did your questions get answered? How about your personal phone line? Did anyone (else) pick up? Was there an option to reach someone else (since you didn't answer) who could help the caller?

Unless all your answers are "Yes," now you understand how it is to be your company's customer, consumer, supplier, or anyone else who wants to (ideally) buy something from your company.

Every interaction with your audiences (customers, suppliers, consumers, the media, prospective employees) is a sales opportunity. It can also be a sales prevention program (see Chapter 38) if it's not done well…over and over.

In almost every case in my career, we did the following (and it boosted sales and our reputation):

1. We hired enough human beings to answer the phone. The consultants will tell you texting, voicemail, web Q&A, and less people saves money and time. It will, in some cases, but being a consumer goods company, it also means you lose every opportunity to truly understand your customer's/supplier's/consumer's issues and correct them. When you do that consistently with people, it leads to more sales. Every time.

2. We trained and rewarded (for good results) our customer service/billing/shipping/technical phone people. These people quickly learn your products, the issues, and what customers want. It's also a good training experience and turns into more sales, both on the phone and if and when they go into the field.

3. We encouraged our managers to call the company. In fact, one of our division presidents routinely called customer service worldwide to check on the performance of his teams. The word got out. He even gave bonuses to those who impressed him. Call answer rates and response time went up and up!

So if you want to understand how and why your company's audiences feel the way they do, call your company. Most of what you need to know is on the other end of the line!

CHAPTER 22

Leadership—Are You Ready?

So you want to be the leader?

Do you believe you have what it takes?

Are you ready?

They say, "Everyone wants to be in charge."

The thing is, it's not true. What is usually true is people only want to do what they (believe the company should do or they) want to do.

Leadership is different. It is a mostly thankless, criticized, questioned, ignored (if possible), lonely, and risky place.

Good leaders are trusted, guide (versus dictate) their teams and companies, build solid relationships, and deliver simple but effective strategies, plans, and results. Leadership by example is very effective.

How do you get ready? Some learnings:

1. Some people believe they are born leaders. Maybe. Most learn from experience, situations, opportunities, and especially other leaders.
2. You study leaders in person. Observe. Learn. Volunteer.
3. Educate yourself. Read about leaders of all types.
4. Ask for leadership opportunities. A lot. Any kind.
5. Find mentors who are successful leaders.

Finally, try it!

Are you comfortable? Are you effective? Do people respond to you? Can you effectively communicate (written and verbal)?

It takes commitment, being unselfish, sharing, and trustworthy.

Why do you want to be a (the) leader? Really? If it's just for ego and/or money, okay, but know everyone will figure that out quickly. Most likely, your leadership days will be numbered. Also, don't confuse artificial leadership (forced due to family or financial power reasons) with real leadership.

If you still want to be a leader, then you have already started—reading this! Now, get going, your new team is waiting.

PS Some very good books on leaders and leadership:

- Grant (Chernow)
- Lincoln (Donald)
- Margaret Thatcher (Thatcher)
- Truman (McCullough)
- Warfighting (USMC)
- Art of War (Tzu)
- The Goal (Goldratt)
- Washington (Chernow)
- Marcus Aurelius (Needleman and Piazza)
- Semper Fi (Ricks)
- Elizabeth I (Starkey)
- Victor, not butcher (Bonekemper)
- Creative Management (Marsteller)

CHAPTER 23

Why You Drop Greedy Customers and Suppliers

It just keeps happening despite your investment of time, money, product development, or trust—certain customers and/or suppliers keep costing you sales and, more importantly, profits.

Yes, they could be poorly managed or are not competitive, but most likely, they are just greedy. Many retailers and/or suppliers have their day where they have an advantage in the marketplace and charge for such situations. These, however, are usually short lived. It's hard to accept, but some customers and/or suppliers are just greedy. They push the limits of good business practices, drive pricing and programs to unrealistic levels, and continually capitalize on weaknesses in their partners.

This may work for a while, but long term, it will fail. The real issue for you is how much cost is there to you and your company if you are partnering with such a company. With customers, it starts with over-aggressive pricing and programs but then works its way into unsubstantiated deductions, fees, freight allowances, returns, rebates, co-op ad costs, and finally, made-up refunds. With suppliers, it's usually price increases due to claimed raw materials, overtime, change fees, product/service design changes, and finally, flat-out pricing for pricing's sake (greed).

What can you do when you find yourself/organization in this situation?

Good business practices (which your customer/supplier is not following) would dictate you do the following:

1. Meet with your customer/supplier and discuss the situation. Use facts. Provide details/costs. Explore why this is happening. The answer most likely will be blamed on their "company needs/policies," and you will not resolve the issues.
2. Elevate the situation to their senior management with one of your senior managers. Explain to your contact this is necessary to reach a "better understanding." Know this will create conflict and possibly threats from your contact(s). Still, losing money to greedy partners is not a long-term strategy.
3. Be prepared to resist these extra charges even if it means loss of some business.
4. Develop alternative products/services you can substitute with your customer/supplier to improve your financials in the short term.
5. Determine your loss of selected or all business with this customer/supplier. Try to set new pricing (which will most likely be rejected) as an exit strategy to give both your company and theirs a transition out.

In the end, you will most likely exit this business. My experience, over and over, is sooner is much better than later. Hope is not a strategy, remember? (See Chapter 4)

You "drop" these types of customers/suppliers because not only are they most likely failing but you will too (in relation to your joint business).

In every case when we followed this approach, we improved our financials, reduced all the extra time and expenses to deal with the "greedy" groups, and built better business with others. Yes, it's difficult short term, but if it's not working now and hasn't for a while, it will most likely get worse.

Let your competitors pay the greedy!

CHAPTER 24

The Fitness Reward

The hard-charging manager, working up to twelve hours a day. Well-caffeinated. Lunch on the run. Lots of travel. Weekends. Leftover vacation days. Not enough time in the day. Is that you?

How do you feel? Are you happy with your mental and physical condition? Are you really productive? Sharp? What are your friends, family and/or significant other trying to tell you? How about your coworkers?

How "fit" are you? Not only physically but mentally? If all the answers are good, then skip this chapter. My guess, however, is that is not the case (you are reading this chapter still…).

Fitness is a process, a commitment, a habit. Your well-being is worth an hour a day, don't you think? If you are not exercising regularly, getting enough sleep, and eating "right," then it won't matter how many hours you work—you will be less productive, healthy, and happy.

It's a result I've seen over and over again. You say you want to exercise, eat right, and get enough sleep but it's just impossible. The job, commute, family, social activities, and travel and financial demands put it last on the list. Okay. Again, how do you feel? Is the job going the way you want? How about everything else? Not good?

So then, how can you do it all? First of all, you can do it all, especially getting and staying fit. It's a matter of balance and commitment. It's also believing in your total life, one that will make everything better if you are fit (well-rested, physically fit, and healthy).

Let's look at a path to better fitness.

1. Assuming you get seven to eight hours of sleep a night, you have at least sixteen hours a day to work with.
2. You need 1 to 1.5 hours a day to exercise—that gives you at least 14.5 hours more.
3. Even the most demanding jobs can be managed in ten hours a day. Let's say two more hours for commuting. (If less, even better. If not, *move closer!*)
4. You still have two to three hours a day to be with the family, socialize, and eat! Minus commuting, you are up another hour.
5. Use your weekends better! You can easily knock out some key projects, e-mails, and calls on Saturday or Sunday mornings before things get going. Organize your week every Sunday morning.

Right about now, you're thinking you have parents, a doctor, and even a personal trainer for such "advice." Well, why isn't it working then? No time? I don't accept that, and neither should you.

Question? What are you currently doing when you do exercise? Is it what you like? Is it running, hiking, walking, yoga, Pilates, team sports, swimming, or biking? Or is it golf, tennis, skiing, or fishing? They don't count in my book! They are events. They are fun but usually are not consistent workouts. So let's develop a real fitness plan:

1. Determine what type of exercise you like.
2. Find a place and/or equipment where you can do that exercise. Don't waste a lot of time getting there. (How about at your house, neighborhood, or at your work at noon?)
3. Commit to the best time of day. Lock it in. (People will get used to it and plan around it. Trust me, they will.)
4. Do it at least five times a week.
5. Eat well…all the time. It makes a big difference. You know smoking, drinking too much, and other such activities do

not promote well-being. You don't sabotage your company, so why do it to your body?

Do this for a week. Adjust. For a month. Adjust. Then do it forever.

Here's what I found in forty years of such an approach:

1. It really works. When you are fit, you do better at everything. The opposite is also true.
2. People will give you the time. In fact, they will admire you for it. You just have to give yourself the time first!
3. We tend to treat our possessions and family better than we do ourselves (our body, mind, and spirit). Prioritize your health first.
4. Know that the cost of being unfit is very high versus your time and expense to be fit.
5. If you want to succeed and be happy, then get the "fitness reward" (physical and mental health), and it will provide what you want in many areas.

That's it. So get up right now and get going.

CHAPTER 25

Great Presenters versus Great Performers

Effective business and especially sales presentations by a great presenter are something to experience. Many times, these presenters are so good you find yourself buying into something you don't want, don't need, or are suspect about. Nevertheless, you can't help yourself. You're in!

The question here is, Do you really believe it? Are you sure you want to buy, invest, or approve?

The challenge is, Do you know if this great presenter can or has delivered as is promised in the presentation? Have you done any due diligence? Do you know if this person and their presentation plan has a successful track record?

All this, of course, is only half the equation. The more important part, regardless of the skill of the presenter, is will this action by you be successful with this particular presenter? Do you trust the presenter?

Here's my learning: Do not assume great presenters are great performers and vice versa. It's a very easy trap to fall into. It's like movie stars versus someone else you don't know. The movie star wows you. The other person, especially if they don't present well but have a good track record, can be overlooked. Bang. You just got wowed... and it most likely will cost you.

It's been my experience to avoid the movie star presenters who rarely deliver on those promises. They unfortunately can make it to the VP level before they are found out. Even then, most people do not want to admit they have been taken in, so the Great Presenter rolls on.

At my last company, we had several Great Presenters at many levels. Usually well-educated, big company (corporate) backgrounds, slick presenters, great at politics, well-dressed, complimentary of you, and promise everything you need!

Problem, however, is they rarely deliver. It's never "their" fault. Their political ties are strong, their fan club even stronger. They also routinely move jobs fast enough to avoid true audits of their performance. Eventually, the "facts" finally tell a story of failure.

Now, however, some great presenters are also great performers. Great! Buy, invest, hire, and approve. Most presenters, however, are not both. So how do you avoid the Great Presenter/political experts from hurting you and/or your company?

Some approaches:

1. Take off your movie star glasses. See clearly. Ask the tough questions. Get answers.
2. Check out their claims, track records, and previous results.
3. Talk to people who worked with or for the Great Presenter. Supervisors will not be a good source. They already have been taken in!

Great Presenters and presentations are fun…like a good movie. Great Performers and solid results are much more profitable. So move the Great Presenters, not results, on to someone else's movie!

CHAPTER 26

There Is (Usually) a Reason That Job Is Open

My great-grandmother, an astute and successful business-woman, taught me several life lessons at an early age. The one I remember best, however, was most "open" jobs are open for a (good) reason.

The real eye-opener here is it doesn't matter what job, company, pay, requirements, or even what century or decade it is; frequently, open jobs have issues!

You say that, but that's how you get a job or new job. That's true. The lesson here is to make sure you do your homework before taking that job. This sounds like Job 101, I know, but you would be surprised how many rational, intelligent, and talented managers rush into a new job without making sure they understand the new job's compensation history, reporting structure changes, and turn-over rate.

We can all get emotionally involved in a job change or be tempted by more compensation (Is it real? Has it been achieved by any other previous managers?) and/or buy into the new company (versus the actual job).

So what can you do? Plenty!

1. Ask to speak to or get contact information for the previous manager(s).
   - Why did they leave?

- Is the compensation right?
- Is the job structured to succeed?
- How was the supervisor?
- Is it budgeted correctly?

2. Ask to speak to some other managers at the company who interact with this job.
    - Is the job needed?
    - Why?
    - What happened to the last manager?

3. Ask the HR department how the last two managers in the job did in the compensation (bonus/commissions) program.
    - What do they think the keys to success are in this job?

4. Investigate "like" jobs at other companies.
    - Compensation similar?
    - Organization approach similar?
    - Do they have similar frequent openings?

5. Reset your emotions. Take a step back; look at the facts and what you have just learned during your investigation. How do you truly feel now?
    - Ask your life team for input. (See Chapter 61.)

Now you know a lot more about why the job is open. This is your career. Make your decision. If it's good overall, great. Go for it. If not, remember what my great-grandma said, "There's a reason that job is open!"

Pay the Army in Gold

Great businesses, like successful armies, operate best with trusted leadership, efficient and fast supply chains, proven strategies, effective performers, and good to great rewards and recognition for their accomplishments.

As a famous Roman general and emperor said, "The secret to success is keep your army's stomachs full and pay them in gold."

Most of the time, businesses do not really understand or follow his advice. The overwhelming greed of most business owners and/or senior management continues to withhold the "spoils" from their armies, rationalizing too much, too soon will create short-term issues (turnover, productivity loss, short-term thinking, and management) while, of course, such thinking creates these very issues due to the "lack" of rewards for *yearly* performance.

In every case in the companies I managed, we were able to change the culture and performance and achieve faster positive financial returns by following the Roman emperor's advice.

You see, "pay for performance," actually means companies do *pay* for improved performance for all the soldiers (employees)…all the time. Private owners, boards, consultants, investors, and especially senior and (bonus) eligible management like to reward themselves handsomely but rarely all the troops. Costly consultants, surveys, industry "norms," and rating agencies (public companies) all jump in to help the top one percent keep the gold in the tower. Yes, I eventually was one of those senior managers. My goal, however, was always to reward everyone, to be the Roman general. It was and remains a challenge, virtually like pushing the elephant "in the room" *up* the mountain!

Still, it can be done. It works. Everybody wins. It takes absolute commitment by management and belief in the approach. All things considered, rewarding everyone for better performance works better than any individual strategy, plan, test, or change in products, channels, or pricing.

I have seven (straight) company examples over thirty years. Everyone worked. The owners, in every case, also made more money than their best (previous) plans, regardless of the extra payouts for the troops.

So how do you do this?

1. Develop a simple compensation plan that rewards everyone for improved financial performance (EBITDA/free cash flow the best).
2. Expand bonuses to everyone. In addition, increase sales department payouts a lot for key performance metrics.
3. Adopt this goal: "Do better this year versus last year." Stop the what ifs, the issues due to this or that. "Better every year"—that's the mantra.
4. Expand and shorten the vesting of all stock programs. (If you want the troops to fight harder, make them all owners of the gold!)
5. Recognize and celebrate accomplishments…all the time.
6. Post-performance by division, by department, by plant, etc., *every month* for everyone to see. You accomplish what you measure.
7. Create this revenue sharing to include your union employees as well. This can be done outside their contracted rates and agreements. We did it. It works. Want record output? Cost improvement? Pay them for their "extra" efforts, and the resulting company improves results. Magic!
8. If you have to, use the current bonus pool, 5–10 percent of the total, to get everyone included. Your bonus man-

agement employees will see the benefits after the first year you do this. Their bonuses will go up in year two (over 100 percent) thanks to the efforts of the entire team.

9. Consider offering the option of no salary increases in trade for larger payout in the bonus programs. We did it. It worked very well. (Not everyone did it at first; some were skeptical and thought 1–3 percent guaranteed raises were better than 3-6 percent bonus payout…until they missed those bonus payments.)

10. If your team, company, and/or owners absolutely block this approach, know this: Your opportunity to get "paid for performance" is most likely very small. It's also why most companies do not make their bonus. You might want to rethink why you work there.

That's it. Everyone together. Pay and recognize the army, and see the gold!

MANAGEMENT CHALLENGES AND SOLUTIONS

Russian Dolls

You want to build your organization?

Get a set of Russian dolls. Open them up. You will notice there is one inside another inside another inside another.

Line 'em up.

See that large doll? Then the next? And the next smallest…to the smallest one.

Let's think about this. Most managers—especially senior managers—think of themselves as the large doll. And when they go to build an organization, they hire someone almost as good as they are. What happens next is that person he hired hires someone almost as good as them and so on down the line…to the point you have an organization as big and talented as the smallest doll.

What you really want to do is to think of yourself as the smallest doll. Always hire someone better, faster, smarter than you…especially in disciplines you are not as familiar. Encourage your organization to do the same. Then add training, evaluation, reward and recognition programs.

Build the organization of the large doll. You are not the best at everything!

I learned the "dolls approach" from a manager when I was in the sporting goods business. I was young—in my mid-thirties—and was not very tolerant of others who I thought were too slow or not smart enough or couldn't provide the performance or the answers needed.

Nevertheless, he called me in one day, and he said, "Have you ever seen my Russian dolls?"

And I said, "No."

My initial reaction was *Why am I in here looking at dolls? I have work to do!*

He slowly took them apart. Talked about those Russian dolls. How many there were. How he got his first set, and then he started to explain to me what I just explained earlier. And that was most people don't have the capacity to think beyond themselves and what's good about them and what's not good about them...the *dolls* do. "If you can," he said, build an organization while thinking of yourself as a small doll, what's on their plate before yours, what are the things you need to get bigger and bigger dolls to get bigger and bigger results." It could be in any department, division, region. Even a department manager can do this; a plant manager can do this; a head of finance can do this.

He said, "If you could do that—if you could really work on this—you will be shocked how well you will do and how well your organization will do."

In every case I did this, it worked.

CHAPTER 29

Compensation and Organization
Drive Behavior—Period

This subject is something I have focused on a lot about in my career, and I actually learned it from the same gentleman who showed me the Russian dolls (see Chapter 28). That is, how you organize people and then compensate them does drive what they are going to do and how they are going to do it. We would like to think everyone willingly fights for their country, that they will do the unselfish thing for the betterment of their company, that they think of their family first, and that their friends are as important to them than their own welfare.

Rarely have I ever seen these things actually happen!

It doesn't mean it doesn't happen from time to time, but if you are driving a large organization, especially in a turnaround or a challenging situation, keep in mind if you organize people for success in a very simple way and compensate them for the behavior you want, that's what you are going to get. And if you don't quite understand that, think about sales forces. How do they make the most money? How do they get the most rewards? They usually sell what they make the most on, period. Your bonus MBOs, I bet you know them by heart! Your total compensation, you work to maximize.

Some things to focus on:

1. Simplify your organization. Eliminate matrix, layers, and group management (not possible? Yes, it is—it's called one person, a COO).

2. Decentralize sales, service, operations, and marketing by business to create the competitive edge you need. Some businesses can utilize shared services (HR, corporate finance, legal, and IT but not anything else).

3. Organize to match your channels and competition. Products change; you can adapt them to shifting channels/customers.

4. Develop realistic financial/sales/EBITDA goals. I usually say, "Better than last year." The bonus prevention programs loved by PE/VC owners or corporate leaders who believe in giant goals usually produce "worse than last year" results. Why? The team knows they are unattainable. Owners/boards/CEOs who actually believe they are "saving" bonus money with unattainable compensation programs demoralize the team and encourage turnover of your best people.

5. Use simple metrics, ones everyone can understand. We once acquired a billion-dollar division. I sat down with fourteen senior leaders and asked them to explain their bonus program. They could not. It was too complex, had to wait until over ten metrics were counted, etc. The effect on behavior was universal. Confusion. Lack of direction. Little feedback. Unintended results.

6. EBITDA/cash flow—In my opinion, it's the best senior management program. Proved it seven times. Where's sales? Where are the MBOs? Where's ROI? Where are all those things you will need consultants for? They are all in there. EBITDA/cash flow. Really. Remember, the sales department has sales in their goals. Everyone, remember, is in sales. No sales, not much EBITDA or cash flow. Simple, easy to understand. You see it every month. Keeps the focus on.

7. Be better every year. Pay better every year. My favorite owner/investor said it best: "The more money Lumley (and his team) makes, the more money I make." That's it. It takes the whole team to build a great company. Everybody wins, not just a small group.

8. Share the spoils. It took a while for the management group to get it, but my companies also shared the bonus pool with factory, distribution, home office, virtually everyone. We carved out a portion of the pool and shared it. Do you think that helped us make twenty quarters in a row before I retired? Sure did. It will work anywhere, even with unions (we paid those workers too, no union add-on in the contracts, record cost improvement and delivery performance in the plants every year).

9. The tougher the task, the more important the compensation. Rome ruled the world for six hundred years. Simple compensation. Gold for winning battles. Everyone shared the spoils.

10. You can also dictate behavior as well with individual departments. Think goals like 25–50 percent EBITDA/cash flow. The rest on their specific areas—sales, operations, etc.

The most important part of the path to success is compensation. Spend the time necessary, and do not get bullied into agreeing to unrealistic goals or a complex plan.

A good plan is everyone wins. If not, go work where it is that way. Yes, only pay for performance (increased EBITDA and cash flow, maybe sales), but get that plan right.

The other models (owners keep it all) decimate companies and their best people.

Like the Romans, armies with full stomachs and gold in their pockets conquer the world!

CHAPTER 30

You Can Beat Anyone

A famous college football coach once said, "How can you expect us to beat them? They are bigger, faster, have more all-Americans, more money, a better school reputation, and a legendary coach." Then they did it...twice.

History is full of such stories and events. The American colonists versus mighty Great Britain. The "Miracle on Ice" USA hockey team. An upstart little store named Wal-Mart versus the mighty Sears.

So why can't your company do the same? You can. You can beat anybody, any company, competitor, product, etc. You just need to figure it out. Focus on the task, all in.

Why are they winning? What are their strengths? More importantly, what don't they do well? Some important tasks first:

1. Go talk to their customers, consumers, suppliers, analysts, and employees.
2. Test those findings.
3. Look for the gaps between you and them. Fundamental, you say; well, have you actually done this? When?
4. Put together a team to be your competitor. What are you worried about if you are them? Is there an opening in the IP? Supply chain? Spending? Concentration in certain retailers, channels, suppliers, consumer groups?
5. Can you grow in areas they dare not go or defend? Of course there is. Find them.

6. Develop claims versus their products. Create a better reason to buy for your product or company versus theirs. Example: a battery that lasts as long for less price. Dominate the value segment/get trial.
7. Celebrate every win versus them. Compensate your people for winning.
8. Identify their cash cow product(s), businesses, or services. Hit them there to distract them while you go after the true targets.
9. Work hard to be mentioned or considered when they are in the media or promotions or trade shows. Make it them or *you*.
10. Have some real fun. Giants fall to the quick, the speedy, and those who are smarter.

You can beat anyone. One battle at a time. Be relentless. Win.

CHAPTER 31

The Five Steps

How did I learn to lead turnarounds at troubled companies? First, by listening to others who did it. Next, by developing simple plans that everyone could understand and execute. Then by actually doing those things I learned from others and those I learned along the way. In addition, I spent a lot of time identifying and recruiting (mostly internally) those people best suited for the task. (Traits included being resilient, team oriented, having unique strengths, being natural leaders.) I learned about the five-step process from a very unique and enlightened president I worked for when I was younger (the Russian Dolls guy! See Chapter 28). He taught me there are five critical steps to fixing a company or brand or product line. They are as follows:

1. Develop a simple vision with your team.
2. Support the vision with a simple strategic plan.
3. Build a simple, streamlined organization and compensation plans.
4. Execute simple action plans quickly.
5. Reward and recognize success.

Sounds simple. Good. It's supposed to be that way. How many leaders, teams, or organizations actually do this and/or do it well? Very few. Why? It's difficult. In times of chaos, there is plenty of blame to go around. What is needed is to get moving...in a new somewhat or totally different direction (see "Just Go That Way," Chapter 36).

It takes leadership. It requires teamwork and buy-in (commitment by the teams). And you must secure upper management and/or ownership support.

Let's talk about the five-step process:

1. *Vision.* Get input from numerous sources, from the board (if appropriate) to the "natural leaders" (see Chapter 14) in your organization. Then get together and develop and agree on your vision (for the company, brand, etc.) Who are you? What do you want to be? How? When? Why?
2. *Strategic plan.* How are you going to do it? Keep it simple. Straightforward. Realistic. Assume little new money available. Remember, your competitors are also doing this. So make sure you do a competitive analysis. (This is an area wherein consultants can help!) Can you capitalize on any of your functions (supply chain, suppliers?) or brands (not being used?) or market segments or channels or geographical areas? Elementary, you say. Then why aren't you doing it?
3. *Organization and compensation.* (See Chapter 29!) Most likely a reorganization to a simpler approach will be needed. Focus on accountability and more direct lines of responsibility. Eliminate as many groups, matrices, and management layers as possible. Develop a simple compensation program directly tied to your vision and plan. It must be realistic.
4. *Execute action plans.* Agree on plans; break those plans into realistic but faster stages of execution. Track weekly. Stay on it. Don't overload your teams with constant changes, additions, and meetings. Such complexity will paralyze the organization. In almost every case of companies I joined that were struggling, either as an operator or board member, this overloading of the operation was a big issue. Very smart CEOs and boards (with their consultants) can't

help themselves. Complicated plans with too many strategies and costs will keep coming your way if you don't get to your five steps quickly. You and your team can do it. Consultants, in most cases, usually really slow down this process. They are smart people but are not in the real fight. Speed and commitment are the key here. Stay in formation; follow the plan (see Chapter 2).

5. *Reward and recognize success.* Building momentum is very important. The new vision, plan, and organization will take some time, so celebrate victories and frequently recognize the winners in team meetings. Reward teams with small bonuses and/or events, dinners, sports tickets, etc. It works. Always has, always will. Most importantly, pay your team at the end of the year if they do better than before. Build on it. No bonuses mean no growth. That sword cuts everyone…and not in a good way.

That's it. Five steps. One after another. Every one important. Get climbing!

They Said the Same Things to Me

"You are so special." "Really like your suit." "Thank you so much for including me." "What a great car." "You look great today." "I really enjoy working for you." "I believe you are the best manager here…"

Then "You are one of our high potentials." "You are on your way." "That promotion is right around the corner." "What a future you have!" "We just need you to do this for me/us."

Whether it's your employees, your supervisors, business friends, or even the board of directors, know this: Beware not to fall into the trap of self-adoration based on people's comments.

As I told a good VP of mine, who was getting a lot of attention since his promotion, "Do you really think that all of a sudden, everyone loves you, or is it what you can do for them?"

Chilling, I know. It is true; however, most of the time, the problem for you is that you start (want) to believe it's all true. You are really something now, better now than everyone else. Then it starts. The decline in your performance.

You are being manipulated. Remember what got you that promotion. Fundamentals. Hard work. Leadership. Being smart. Being yourself. Keep things in perspective. Stay grounded.

Why? Well, you see, those types of people, they said the same things to me…

Change Is Good (As Long as It Doesn't Affect You)

If only we could change (fill in the blank), things would be better. We usually believe we do know a better way to do most things. If only "they" could see it.

Perhaps we also feel certain people in the organization need to go, be moved, be better trained, and/or (especially) talked to about their performance, style, communications, client interaction, and/or (fill in the blank).

With regard to the company, how about senior management decisions, strategy, investments, plans, products, brands, customers, certain divisions, compensation, advertising, benefits, political support, offices, benefits, or (fill in the blank)?

Most of us do believe, if we could just get "them" to change, things would be so much better, especially for you! You know, many times, you and/or the majority are right. The thing is, most people also feel the same way, but instead, they believe you or your department, division, or team needs change.

So here we are. Let's say, however, which is usually the case, things and/or people do need to be changed. Unless company performance and all employee performance is maximized, change is needed. You can participate in or be a bystander of such change.

Change is constant. We all know this! We want it to happen, but that also usually carries the big condition that is "as long as it doesn't affect you" in any negative way.

Many believe Darwin said evolution is about "the survival of the fittest." What he actually said was "It is not the strongest of the species that survives nor the most intelligent but the one most responsive to change."

Change can be good. It means we are evolving, adapting. The negative, toxic, and greedy leaders who change things for the worse sooner or later fade away. It is the team approach, the we-are-all-in-this-together change we all participate in that works. It enables companies to improve, to adapt. Company after company I was part of experienced many of these challenges, usually caused by poor company leadership and lack of positive change. Just one person can bring down entire businesses, divisions, products, stock prices, and employee performance.

The same is true the other way around. One person can affect positive change even if it affects you. You and then the next person, then the next, and so on changes things. Momentum, they say, goes both ways. My experience has been it's much easier to turn companies the wrong way than the right way, but once the team buys in and adapts, then things can be energized positively for the long term.

That means success.

Now we could go through numerous examples of how the ability to change leads to company success, but perhaps how to get it started is more important.

Here's how our teams did it:

1. Listen/ask what is working and not working.
2. Communicate your findings to everyone in person.
3. Tell the truth.
4. Develop a plan to change to what is needed to be done.
5. Communicate the plan in person to everyone, from company-wide meetings, one-on-ones, departments, divisional meetings, union meetings, plants, distribution centers, to sales meetings.
6. Do what you say when you say.
7. Celebrate change and its victories.
8. Reward and recognize the positive change leaders.

9. Keep all audiences in the loop on the change progress.
10. Personally participate in the change process and its positive and negative impacts.

Everyone wins when everyone embraces positive change. Be the leader.

CHAPTER 34

Leverage Is Everything

What is leverage in business? It's usually the difference between winning or losing in almost every situation, especially conflicts. Leverage is achieved in many ways.

It can be bought (ownership), inherited, earned, or developed or even through perception.

If your company has a principal owner, they have a lot of leverage (to get what they want done). Your boss has leverage over you (authority, your job, pay, title, etc.). Your largest customer (as most customers) has leverage over your company (sales, distribution, profits). Your company has leverage over your suppliers. On and on it goes.

Now there are exceptions where leverage can be reversed. Your owners really want something they can't mandate. Your company has the hottest product in the market, and your customers must have it. Your boss really needs you. Here, leverage is a powerful tool to help you achieve your goals.

Some lessons learned about leverage:

1. It usually is time sensitive. When you have it, best to use it before things change.
2. It is a knife that cuts both ways, so use it carefully, knowing it could be you on the other end next time.
3. Don't overestimate how powerful it is if you're dealing with a high-ego individual, as they may become emotional and react irrationally, creating new problems.

4. Consider using your advantage in a manner the other side has options and can rationalize accepting your proposal (via your leverage).
5. Be confident in and committed to your advantage and proposal or risk losing your leverage.

Achieving sustained leverage is something best learned from both sides of the table. Consider the issues from several points of view. This means, use your leverage when you really need it. If you don't have any leverage, then work hard to develop it. If you do have leverage, work hard to keep it. How?

Leverage is the power—you usually need to build it from a position of strength.

1. What are your personal strengths at your job? Company?
2. What are your company's strengths? Especially versus the competition?
3. What is unique and/or very difficult to replace or find that only you or your company possess?

Develop and refine these strengths. Build them into a position of power and leverage.

Why? You will most likely have to have leverage to win and achieve some of your most important goals or needs. You will certainly want to have leverage in conflicts, as many such events get resolved based on who has the most leverage.

Now having leverage in a conflict is one thing; using it is another. Make sure you are committed to using it, or you will most likely lose the conflict but also the leverage itself.

Here are a few real-life examples:

1. The Kitchen Appliances Seesaw
    We had two major brands in a very large retailer. New Asian brands, and more importantly, the retailer's private label itself, became major competitors, reducing our distribution and pricing. Our ability to grow (and even hold)

our business was under siege. Then an opportunity to shift the leverage seesaw presented itself. To achieve this shift, we had to move very fast. The retailer lost their key appliance dedicated store brand license (another story). We had a third brand, not being used for appliances but in the store for other non-appliance products. In a call between their chief merchant and us (myself), we had a weekend to tip the seesaw. This is how fast leverage can change (especially if you constantly pursue it). We would "give" our third brand to the retailer to use for their exclusive store brand if they would hold and increase our appliances distribution (assuming our products sold through well). Win-win. More importantly, the leverage shifted. We now had leverage versus little to declining before.

2.   The Money Game

All of the last four companies I was at were in very difficult financial situations when I arrived and/or was put in charge. The compensation programs were ineffective. The employees, especially key ones, were leaving for several reasons but mostly due to poor compensation. (Yes, it's usually about the money.) Recruiting top new people (for the same reasons) was also close to impossible. Still, ownership and/or the board wanted standard compensation programs with high targets. Boards in denial is a very prevalent problem among poor performing companies and divisions. You see, it is that very board and/or ownership group that bought into the company, its leaders and the strategies that got it into its present (bad) situation. Yes, sometimes market situations caused a lot of issues but not all of them. So how do you fix it? Well, not with an unrealistic compensation plan or the standard one either. It's a creative plan, starting with where the company is at *now*, not where it was or should be or could be. A creative plan, performance-based, mostly separate from the current, shared, or previous plans is the answer. We presented, in each case, the new (leverage) plan: Lose more money and people and still struggle recruiting top talent via the current approach and compensation plan or go with our plan. We "levered" the way back with keeping key people, acquiring new talent, and then rewarding the team quickly for improving results. No big targets. Just improve every quarter. Each year. Use two years (versus four-year long-term programs) at a time.

All four times, it worked. Why?

We followed the leverage plan.

    a.   We had time-sensitive plans.
    b.   We found leverage for our plan.
    c.   We didn't overestimate our leverage.
    d.   We presented options.
    e.   We were committed and confident.

They say there's not just one thing to building a successful plan. They are right. Just make sure you find your leverage; it's not one of those things—it's *everything*.

Ninety Percent of It

Many managers routinely ask, "What are the keys to business success?"

The answers are aplenty. One of the most important keys to business success I believe I learned at an early age.

Some believe 90 percent of life is showing up. That's close. Let's build on that point. My experience was 90 percent of achieving business success was not only showing up but showing up *all* the time. That means never giving up. That means finding a way. That means your persistence to learn, listen, sell, build, achieve, and reach your goals doesn't vary. You keep at it. Getting discouraged, losing out sometimes, not being treated fairly, and a list of other obstacles will test your patience, spirit, and most importantly, your persistence.

You may get plenty of understanding from coworkers, friends, your significant other, and even your boss about why you are not reaching your goal(s). Most people accept that and move on (but not necessarily up!).

Persistence isn't a degree. It doesn't cost money. Persistence is a weapon few can defeat. When you become the most persistent one in the business game, you most likely will succeed. You say there are many persistent people who were wrong. True. My response? Then you have to be more persistent!

Here are some incredible examples:

1. One-on-One Sales

    How about a former AT&T coin telephone salesman who kept going back to every customer he had to sell that last coin telephone until, after three sales calls in the last week, he convinced a butcher shop owner to install the phone in his beef freezer (in case they got locked in)! That salesman made his quota bonus and taught me a lot about persistence. He ran our house with Mom!

2. New Account Distribution

    Our company had a bad experience at the United States' top Big Box hardware store. They kicked our alkaline batteries out—all this before I arrived. We tried everything to get another chance. We explained we were the new team. We provided great pricing, terms, and rebates. We offered free in-store merchandising. We built multi-language displays. Three years of persistence but no success. We/I built relationships throughout the organization, right to the CEO. Two more years. We stayed after it. We then put it all together with our other products, and after five years, we were rewarded. The CEO told us they were never going to let our batteries back in but were impressed with our persistence. Those batteries are still in distribution at the Big Box five years later.

3. That Job

    Many have their eyes on their "dream job." It may be at your current company or another (let's not confuse dream jobs with dream companies). Perhaps you (or others) don't believe you are qualified or will be successful or "fit" for the job (plenty of biases here). So what to do? Go after it!

    - Get some more targeted experience (somehow, somewhere) maybe via a task force, team, non-profit, or volunteer that will help your case.
    - Add outside education if appropriate (like classes or advanced degree.)

- Look for chaos (problems) where the job is or may happen. Make your case; you will take it on.
- Ask your boss to help you…a lot.
- Be persistent!

By the way, this is how I became a director, VP, SVP, and president. That's right. Like the guy who sold the coin telephone to the butcher for his freezer or got batteries into the Big Box after five years and made CEO. Ninety percent of it all was…persistence.

PS The Persistence Meter

1. *You are starving.* Food is over a twelve-foot fence. You don't have a ladder. My bet: *You figure it out.*
2. *You are in love.* The other party may get away. I'm sure you did or will *find a way to not lose them!*
3. *You wanted to get a master's degree.* You didn't have the time or money. Somehow *you did it!*

CHAPTER 36

Just Go That Way

Many times, you are faced with what appears to be a really tough task. People use words like "impossible," "no way," or "maybe we should just find a new job!" Most of the time, the main problem is being "frozen in place." So what do you do? Just get going in a new direction, meaning take a good look at the situation. Don't overanalyze it. You don't need consulting firms to tell you you have a problem. You are probably losing money and/or losing market share, margin, and most importantly, customers and consumers. Simply identify the key problems, and stop doing what's causing it. Then "just go that way (a different way)." It doesn't have to be in a straight line. It just has to be that way, sort of, kind of a little left, a little right. Think of a boat swerving left, swerving right, but going in one general direction. Just go one way and you'll start building some confidence, get people on board, and start the process to fixing your problem. Yes, it could be wrong as well, but you have begun the right process. Stopping the big failure. Going a different way. This will get the organization to find the right way.

In everyday business, there are a lot of less critical examples, but in a crisis and/or turnaround situation, you need to change right away. As I've said before, just quit doing what you've been doing. This will help everyone get over the depression and the feeling of hopelessness. Identify the issues. You can borrow from the big cheese approach. Identify a few things you want to do. Tell the people you are going a new way. For instance, you are not going to sell five thousand types of shoes anymore; you are now going to sell just one thousand because those one thousand shoes represent 80 percent of your sales and profits. You are not going to sell to these certain customers anymore; you are only going to sell to a few where you make money. You are not going to sell to these international markets anymore; you are only going to sell to a select few where you have better opportunities. You may launch something new, you may try new channels of distribution, or you may sell certain items only on the Internet. You may add some new products. Just head in one general direction. Many companies go round and round in circles. That's no direction.

Just go away from what you were doing. Sounds simple. Most people will keep doing what is failing because that's what they know. They hope it will somehow turn around. They are afraid of change. That's why you change. It's the first step to improving things. Just go…that way.

The big PS. In every case we did this—outboard motors, boats, bikes, consumer storage, nutritional products, batteries, kitchen appliances, pet products, home and garden products, men's and women's personal care products, and even international markets—they all improved.

Go in Person

In today's business world, it seems increasingly normal that we try to avoid going to see people or manufacturing plants or retail stores in person. We have phones, cameras, text, Facetime, Zoom, and Blue Jeans (like Zoom!).

Travel, meetings, and one-on-ones in person are time consuming, not "climate" friendly, and costly. Besides, many believe they are more productive staying in the office or working from home. Then there are the health scares and resulting social and physical distancing considerations from time to time.

So how do you get to know someone? See firsthand the plant or stores or consumers in action?

Usually, people learn the most about other people in person. Most people agree on this. We still rationalize why it isn't necessary very often, especially when we get busy or overwhelmed.

Why is it so important to go in person anyway?

My experience and learnings regarding in-person visits all point to the same answer: because it works better. It works because you see, hear, and understand better. You learn things you would never learn any other way. Your instincts are best in person. You can feel it. It energizes you. You are better for it. They get to know you better as well, which helps you (usually!).

· You create personal bonds that bind you and them together better. For instance, you see firsthand how and why the plant is working so well...or not.

Some Lessons

1. *Customer meetings.* Make it a point to go in person, ideally one on one. Cut through the layers. Get the straight story. Build a personal relationship, an understanding. I could write an entire book of examples of success about in person sales meetings. Here's just one:

   - The CEO of one of our largest customers, the biggest US home hardware big box chain, and I were able to meet in person several times over the years. These meetings were usually about difficult business situations. Still, these "in person" meetings built a good amount of trust between us. We saw, felt, and knew we could believe each other. When the company I had recently joined (turnaround) was forced into Chapter 11 (for a brief time), we were able to talk again, one on one, and believe each other, and they decided to support us through that situation. Think all those in-person meetings and the resulting trust between us helped here?

2. *Suppliers.* I recommend you go in person to see what and how your key suppliers and leaders do things. Ask for their input on how your company can do better? Save money? Get faster? They usually want to share this information, and it's better for both organizations. See for yourself if their passion and commitment are to the level you need. In fact, at my last three companies, we hosted a yearly working conference in Asia and Europe for all key suppliers. The rules were simple: They showed us, told us, and worked with us to help them help us. We listened! We also met, in separate meetings with each of them and visited their plants. The results? We routinely achieved and improved cost improvement percentages for COGS from the previous 0 to 1 percent to now 3 to 4 percent...per year.

3. *Your salespeople.* I was taught to get to know my companies' salespeople in person. To listen to their challenges, com-

petitive information, ideas, and what your customers are saying. Do this in person whenever you can. In person, you will get to see, hear, and feel their true passion, emotion, and commitment. They will better believe you can help them which, in turn, better helps you and the company. Not a believer? Try it, then decide.

4. *Company HQ.* Career tip—go in person whenever you can to visit or for specific meetings to your company HQ. Get to know the people in all departments that can help you and vice versa. Build awareness and better understanding of your department and/or division and what is going on. You will need their support sooner or later. They will best remember whom they have met in person.

5. *On-site plant visits.* When you go in person for meetings that are about difficult situations, it provides the opportunity to turn failure into success. At the bike business, we had a key bike frame partner whose business we had directly helped increase fivefold. In fact, they added an entire additional plant. Things were good for both of us until our number one customer (and the world's largest retailer of bikes) requested a rather large price reduction based on competitive alternatives. We went back to all our partners to share these cost reductions with us. Overall, it was progressing well except for the bike frame partner. Finally, I flew to Asia with key team members. Our meeting was civil, the tour long, the lunch longer, the presentation on why they could not afford to help us very detailed. The meeting with the family-run business with the father (owner) and four sons grew contentious. We took a break. I requested a view of the new plant/paint area. They agreed. We departed but were asked to "go around" the alley between the plant buildings. It was going fine until I "cut through" the alley on the way back to the meeting by accident. Parked there were five new BMW luxury sedans. The duty on such cars in Asia usually doubled the cost of each car. Let's call it almost $750,000. We would have never known about this

information from a phone meeting. The meeting resumed. In the next few minutes, I confirmed the cars were theirs (yes). I explained that neither I myself nor my team had company cars or BMW's. So we again repeated our joint business was now very much at risk and they couldn't help but own five new cars. That was it. They agreed to participate. Did they sell the cars? Not sure!

So if there had been no in-person trip, there would have been no BMWs to walk by. Probably no bike cost reduction. Probably significant loss of business at the retailer. It was a long way to Asia and back. It was a much shorter and better trip to the retailer, which we did in person.

6. *Management presence.* While most managers will not be faced with the decision of where to live regularly, many of you may be at certain times in your career. One of the most important lessons I have learned in business and life is "It's impossible to commit to maybe!" (See Chapter 3.) Yet so many senior managers believe they don't have to live where they work (as in, being an in-person leader) or that it is important. "In person" isn't necessary for them. I believe that's not a *big* "Maybe they are not committed" message to the troops. My requirement for my key team was simple: Everyone moves to their assigned office location, especially senior management. We were all there "in person" and together. It really worked for all the obvious reasons. Each company I ran improved and used this approach. Was the "in person" approach the only reason? No. Was it one of the key reasons? Absolutely.

CHAPTER 38

The Sales Prevention Department(s)

Successful selling requires a lot of things to go right. They include product development, manufacturing, performance, cost, pricing, salespeople, order management, delivery, advertising, promotion, billing, sell-through, returns, credit, customer service, regulatory compliance, and profits for all concerned.

Anywhere along the sales process, a bottleneck or bump-in-the-road can happen. Delays. Risk of cancellation. Sales lost, missed, or substituted with less profitable items.

All this is the result of doing business inefficiently or poorly. Still, what you really don't want is your own organization to hold back or impede sales. In so many companies I joined, the first thing I heard was how difficult it was to deal with our company. Feedback included we had over complex ordering, credit, delivery, and return processes and policies.

Each department in a business is tasked with doing well, being cost efficient, and meeting budgets. Left unchecked, unmonitored, and without customer feedback, these departments can evolve into standalone hierarchies of "sales prevention" (SP).

The IT system (as in the ordering and billing system) is a common department to blame. Adding new channels of distribution (Internet, international, mass, etc.) is another common area of SP. In the end, however, it can be every department. Corporate departments live on their islands, usually unaffected by frustrated customers. The goal then is to get everyone into the sales "invention" program!

How's this?

1. Tie everyone together (comp program) to the sales/ EBITDA number. Everyone now is in sales!
2. Get representatives from every department to meet and talk to your key customers (and sales) to understand how they can stop preventing sales and instead fix their areas to move things along faster and more effectively.
3. Require sales to meet every month (not just quarterly) with forecasting and operations. Better communication means better support departments...and results.
4. Reward sales for more accurate forecasts, just like operations does for their areas.
5. Publish customer input about all departments.
6. Publish forecast and customer delivery goals and results. (You say you do this. Does anyone get credit or called out for the results?)

How about some examples?

1. *Easy one.* A weekend night at your favorite restaurant/bar. Very crowded. There's just one, maybe two, bartender(s). People three deep at the bar plus the dinner table orders. The wait is long. Sales prevention hall-of-fame.
2. *IT system.* Let's say your system was designed for small independent customers or when the company was smaller. Sales now sells mass merchants. Everyone is frustrated. Long delays for input, changes, returns, POS data, etc. Result: cancelled orders. Lost sales and eventually distribution. The entire infrastructure is sales prevention.
3. *Finance.* Your policies may limit credit, returns, and make-goods until your system cycles or can be reviewed overnight or the end of week or month's end. That's sales prevention every day. Outdated policies or system/people appear too slow to your customers. They then buy from your faster competitors.

4. *Political battles.* Department Head A can't stand Sales Department Head, so they make their (sales) life miserable. Great. Sales Prevention Poison Award. This happens all the time. Confront both department heads. Get them to talk and fix it. If not, get their representatives to fix it. Finally, go to the boss. Poor systems can hurt you; fighting people can be worse!

5. *Sales department "over" forecasting.* The biggest sign your organization's entire process is broken is overstating forecasts by sales. Excess inventory everywhere because many departments are too slow, complex, or just flat out not working well enough. Now some salespeople are also not good at forecasting. Train them. Allow for a percentage of over forecasting. Still, call them out with facts. Again, go through points one to four here. Your issues are most likely in there.

Sales prevention can be fixed. Work hard to get all the preventers to become inventors. The result: an entire system of sales providers!

CHAPTER 39

Get It in Writing

Verbal understandings. Agreements. Promises. All common ways of communicating. None, however, will help you very much when there's a misunderstanding, challenged agreement, and/or during or after a broken promise.

Two things two different CEOs taught me:

1. If it's important, get it in writing.
2. Good contracts (written) make good neighbors.

You say that's hard at times. Yes, it is. That's why you need it. It's exactly when someone won't or doesn't want to put your agreement in writing tells you what you need to know: Don't depend on that agreement!

Here are some examples:

1. The Financial Agreement—"You accomplish this, you and your team will get paid this—trust me." This sound familiar? It's usually your superior or even someone with more influence who makes the promise. In this case, it was the key leaders. We achieved our numbers. They changed things on their part. A litany of excuses, from board objections (to communications misunderstandings).

   It created several creditability issues. It was costly for us. It, however, taught us all what we needed to know: Get agreements in writing. From then on, that was the rule. We also knew not trust verbal promises ever again, so everything went to written reports and agreements.

2. The Political Agreement—A lunch invitation. One on one. Time to get to know each other better. This invitation came from a high-ranking person (board member). We had a great discussion. Then the real subject came up. The board member (himself the previous COB) says he (and the board) are hearing things they don't like about the new CEO (whom I reported to). He/they would like to talk more to me about this confidentially. Would I do it?

    I was then thirty-nine years old, first time on a board, and frankly knew the new CEO was a very poor fit for the job and industry we were in. I was also led to believe this "meeting" would never come back on me and I was helping the company and myself.

    The next step was to set the meeting. Meanwhile, I called a mentor of mine and former boss. I explained the situation (and opportunity). He asked just one question: "Did you get these promises about your lack of risk and opportunity in writing?"

    I said, "No, but you don't understand. It was all good."

    He said, "No, it's you who doesn't understand, but you will…"

    I didn't do the next step. It's not in my belief system. Still, I did ask for the promise about my no-risk participation in the lunch (to test the theory) in writing (in case the lunch was used as an implied agreement of supporting the board member's goal: remove the new CEO).

    No written agreement ever appeared. As my mentor said, I understood now. My mentor was, of course, right. If the agreement is not in writing, there's a good chance it's not real and/or you will not get what was promised.

The examples could go on and on:

1. The buyer is your biggest customer who verbally promises more business if you give that big price break.
2. The supplier who verbally promises to give you competitive information (later) for better pricing (as in more) now.
3. The consultant who verbally promises to do this and that for a special fee…now.

In almost all these cases and more, if you don't get it in writing, don't bank on you getting what was agreed to.

So how do you get it in writing? Some approaches:

1. Ask. Then make it clear it's best for both of you.
2. If the other party resists, usually because "it's sensitive" or "not done yet," wait until it can be done. This probably means they cannot deliver.
3. You write up the agreement and get the other party to sign it. (Best to have your lawyer look at it if it is a large deal or if you suspect other possible "issues.")
4. Try to get a third party involved in the agreement, especially on their side. This will test the reality of the agreement.
5. If you can't get the agreement in writing but really have to do it, get others to witness/hear the deal…on both sides. (Still, this is risky.)

A simple way to remember this? How about when you order at a restaurant and the server says, "I can remember this all—I don't have to write it down"? How often does that work out for you?

You get the picture. Get it in writing or get left out.

CHAPTER 40

How to Hire a Great Salesperson

"The more money 'my name' makes, the more money I make" (CEO of PE firm who owned over 50 percent of our stock). Loved that guy!

He understood how to hire great salespeople. Sales is the lifeblood of any company. Great salespeople pump that blood faster.

So how do you find and, more importantly, hire great salespeople? Yes, there is their track record. References. Their interview. Their presentation (see Chapter 25).

How about their results? What do customers say about them? What did people who worked with them say? Did they sell you?

Let's try this another way. Is money they can make important to them?

Why are they in sales? Do they move around a lot? Why?

My experience is that great salespeople are disruptors of your competition, your customers, and most of all, your organization. They need and want things done…now. Why? One, they committed it to their customer. Two, they get paid for it.

The best salesman I ever knew taught me a very easy but telling question to ask your candidates when you want to determine if you should recruit/hire that new salesperson, that is, "How would you like to be paid?"

Confident, successful, and great salespeople will have the same answer: "Full commission rate."

That's because they believe and know that's how they will make the most money. Great salespeople like recognition, but they love money. The more they make, the more you make.

Any other answer says that candidate is really a marketing candidate!

CHAPTER 41

Why You Get Fired

Few people believe they will ever get fired. The thing is, you most likely will get fired at least once in your career. Why?

Two reasons. One, you either underperform, or two, you do too well—that's right—too well. You gain power and a strong following at the expense of your superior(s). This can also lead to extra ordinary income, another issue for those above you.

Performing poorly and being in the wrong job at the wrong company and/or in the wrong industry or boss all lead to parting ways. Sometimes you take a job you know you can't or won't do. Your attitude, if negative, also is a red flag for you. Sometimes managers, subconsciously, want out. Getting fired gets a severance. So things go that way. Try very hard to think about and check all these things before you take the new job!

Doing too well, however, is a very different situation. How do you do a great job and somehow do too well?

This happens, especially in senior management. Power, money, politics, ego, and personalities all converge at the top.

Who's really in charge? Who will get the most credit for success? Who will make the most money? Whose ego is bruised? Who trusts whom? Who isn't trusted? (See Chapter 70.)

In publicly traded companies, this is a bit better than private companies, but companies controlled by private equity investors or families in either case create the most potential issues for the doing-too-well manager.

Why? That manager (you!) may also be doing very well financially, getting the lion's share of credit with the board and/or investors (Wall Street analysts) or the key owner.

This all leads to hidden problems with the doing-too-well leader and one or more others being impacted and/or not listened to or getting as much (more) income and/or credit as you. (See Chapter 65.)

What to do?

1. Work hard to share the credit, regardless of the imbalance.
2. Build a relationship with the people being impacted. This means in person. (See Chapter 37.)
3. Develop an objective understanding with all the other key senior people above you in the situation.
4. Protect yourself in any way you can (severance agreement, outside contacts).
5. Keep doing well. Results are power. It's a lot more difficult to fire the good performer for political reasons unless you give those who want you out or reduced, non-performance-related reasons (emotional outbursts, etc.)

Getting fired is the risk here. Doing well while recognizing and dealing with what is going on is the best defense.

Your job is to do a great job at work and with all those who can (unfairly) impact that job (you) and your team. It's the penalty, at times, of great leadership.

CHAPTER 42

How to Get Hired

Throughout my career, it has always baffled me how many people do not know how to secure interviews, how to prepare for the hiring process, and how to close the deal to get the job offer they desire.

Yes, very few people always succeed in this area. Still, you can be very successful if you put in the time, effort, and creativity to achieve your goals.

Fundamentally, it's the same for a first-time manager as it is for a CEO. Overall, it's preparation, pursuit, practice, creativity, and determination.

This chapter assumes you know the industry, companies, and job title you are pursuing.

Some basic thoughts:

1. Why do you want this job?
2. What do you bring to the job and company? (Why you?)
3. Is this move part of your career plan?
4. Are you willing to do the work to properly prepare for the interviews?
5. Will you be successful for them and you?

If you can't answer these questions directly yourself and convincingly to your life team (see Chapter 61), start again. You are not ready.

If you can answer and convince yourself and others, then let's go get this job!

Here are some steps that usually get you there:

1. Research the company, its competitors, and its customers.
2. Visit its retailers and get input on their company and products (even if only consumers).
3. Revise your resume (CV) to be short and to the point, and list accomplishments primarily. Your resume should be one page, two at the most. Lots of white space (so they can write notes, get involved with you, want to know more).
4. Get a detailed job description from the company and/ or recruiter. Study it. Prepare your answers/strengths (be ready for weaknesses) for all key areas.
5. Talk to others who have had the job or those who have (at like companies). That's not easy, you say. I know. That's why you are going to do it. It will set you apart. Just like the retailer visits and their input.
6. Develop *your* questions for them. What is working? What isn't working? (Basic but still core questions.) Where would they like this job/division/company to be in a year? Two years? What are the top 1–2 things they must have or have happen in this job? Fashion some of these questions to lead back to you, your accomplishments, and your strengths.
7. Persistence is 90 percent of just about everything. Never let up. Stay after it. Emails, texts, articles they might like, calls, stop-bys, accidental (on purpose) meetings, associations, trade shows, clubs. Reach out to their friends, company associates, and especially their assistant. You want this job or not? Yes, it may appear you are overanxious, want the job too much, and are really demonstrating that all the time. Just like you will do when *you* have the job!
8. Practice your pitch and answers...out loud. You are too good, too mature, and won't do this. Okay, you must be an outstanding speaker, interviewee, and candidate. Just wing it...

9. Be creative. This is usually really overlooked in the process. It doesn't matter how you demonstrate your creativity. Before the interview, during, or after. It can be a unique way to get noticed, a creative solution to an issue of theirs, or how you follow up (unique handwritten card tied into your conversation). Creativity is remembered long before line 10 on your resume!

10. Ask for the job. No time to be coy. Great salespeople know how to close. Ask them if you need to, but do it! Be ready when you ask for the job to explain what you will do for them. Trust is important here. Tell them they can depend on and trust you to deliver.

Like school, you need to get an A grade here. That's success on 90–95 percent of these ten points. Sorta like getting married! It's a yes or no (maybe a no).

Get that ring!

All Glory Is Fleeting

You won. Enjoy it for today. Great job.

Tomorrow, next week, month, or year is a new challenge. Past accomplishments are good for a few things—resumes, stories, and learnings—much like college.

Know this: It's behind you. One day, that's your reward.

Now go forward. New, more glory. Every one, a new one.

You are as good at what you did today and perhaps tomorrow.

It takes most people a career to learn this simple truth known throughout time to all warriors: "All glory is fleeting."

How to Leave Your Job the Right Way

You want to get a new job. You have an offer, and you need to tell your boss and your friends at the company. So now what?

It seems easy to everyone but you, or at least they/you believe it should be easy. After all, why else did you put in all the time and effort (and risk) to seek out new employment?

There must be a reason or several of them—opportunity? Compensation? Promotion? Family and/or personal issues? You can't stand your (fill in the blank) at your current job?

Ideally, you have taken the time to objectively (beware of short-term emotions and ego that can rush you into a new job prematurely) consider the pros and cons of your current situation versus the new opportunity. Let's backtrack for a moment. Here's some great input from others and lessons learned about job switching:

1. Until you have a written offer, detailing all key points (title, job description, compensation, benefits, reporting structure, and severance policy), you aren't resigning yet!
2. What's really the key reason you
    a. want to leave your current job?
    b. want to accept this new job?
    Do they match? If not, why not?
3. Does this new position, company, and/or industry meet your long-range plan? (What? You don't have a long-range plan?) Back to start. Develop one right now. If you don't

know where you are going, how will you (ever) get there? If it does (meet your plan), great. Keep going!

4. Have you done your homework? Have you reached out to others about the company, your department, your boss, track records, and especially the person in the job *before you*? What do its customers, suppliers, Wall Street, competitors, etc., think? No? Too excited? Make time right now. Check it out. It's why armies send scouts out first! You don't want to jump right into a similar or even worse situation than you are currently in. You will never be in a better position to check things out than now.

5. Does it feel right? Your instincts (not emotions) are your guiding light here. It's normal to have some apprehension, emotions, fears, etc., about moving on, but deep down, do you "feel" this is right?

Okay, assuming you are (still) ready to move, there is a right way and a wrong way to resign. We all understand "the greener pasture" situation. It's exciting to be the one leaving. It's a statement (hopefully that you are being pursued, on your way up).

The right way to leave is important. Business careers are a long, long race. Everyone you work with, for, beside, or around will (continue) to have an impact on your career one way or another. Recruiters know these people too. They will ask them about you. These people "volunteer" opinions, right or wrong. Objective or not. When you leave, keep this in mind (and forever).

Know this: In more instances than I can count, I got contacted by recruiters and others about people I worked with or for me, sometimes several times. So here are some approaches to consider (and use):

1. You go in person (no text, phone, video) to your superior and explain you have an offer you *are* accepting to join another company. (If your goal is to bargain/leverage your new offer to get more where you are, good luck—it rarely works out long term. You will lose the trust they have in you. Period.)

You thank them for what you have learned, how much you will miss the people and company, and offer (at least) a two-week transition. Also, you assure your superior(s) and team members you will prepare all transition materials, meetings, to-do lists, etc., and then do it very well.

2. Resist the "Ha ha, I'm out of here!" meetings, drinks, talking trash about your bosses, and others. It will not go unnoticed or be forgotten.

3. Remember, you will most likely (someday) need this or these people's references. In fact, you may even work with or for one of them in the future!

4. Your resignation should also be *in writing*. This will serve as an official document in the company and state in *your words* why you left (simple, straightforward message—an offer you couldn't pass on based on your career plan).

5. Going-away parties are nice but a real risk if you decide to do the following:
   a. Drink alcohol.
   b. Start whispers about why you are "really" leaving.
   c. Tell off certain people.

I usually went to such events but drank no alcohol and focused on "them" and good stories about them and how proud I was to be part of their team. Be careful here, very careful.

Finally, consider handwritten notes to key people. Thank them. Offer to be available if they need to reach out to you. It will pay dividends forever.

Now, you ask, what not to do? Easy, don't do everything opposite of the How to Leave Your Job the Right Way we just outlined.

CHAPTER 45

R&D: The Hidden Opportunity

Research and development. Just the words scream technical processes, people, and "hope" spending. It's also the "old school" designation for today's technology department.

Still, good companies grow through new products, processes, product/service performance enhancements, and complimentary offerings the R&D department develops. Such work is important and necessary. It is also usually expensive with no guarantees of success.

Still, it's here, I have found, most companies, owners, and leaders miss a great opportunity—that being R&D has many more contributions and uses than just research and development.

The very processes, testing, specifications, manufacturing ability, costs, and performance characteristics that make up initial and existing products over time are rarely challenged, improved, or radically changed. Yes, big sellers or non-competitive products get attention (usually out of absolute necessity), but the vast number of SKUs get little attention and review. Why? It's not really R&D's job? It's too time consuming? R&D has better things to do? R&D doesn't have the budget or resources? Probably all true, especially based on the way companies budget. Marketing budgets? Up! Sales? Up! Administrative costs? Up! Travel? Up! R&D budgets? Cut!

Here's the secret. R&D is one of your most powerful and productive product and company-wide cost savings departments. Those resulting savings will more than pay for the use of R&D resources but also can help fund more marketing and sales spending. Really? Absolutely.

At each consumer goods company I led, this was one of the first areas to capitalize on. Want more marketing funds? They are sitting in your product line SKUs. You don't believe it? (See Chapter 11.)

Here's what we did over and over:

1. Analyzed our product line for 80/20 SKU sales and gross margin.
2. Established an R&D task force to study the 80/20 product line
   - Colors (Why so many?)
   - Specifications (Still needed at current levels?)
   - Sizes (Still need them all?)
   - Packaging (Too much?)
   - Time from manufacturing order to deliver to customer (Has it been reduced? If not, reduce the time and with it, the inventory.)
3. Reduce all appropriate SKUs and streamline, reengineer, and simplify processes. Shift to the speed model. Get it done.
4. Have R&D ask your suppliers how to do this same exercise as well (their ideas to improve all).
5. Study your product POS data at your top customer. Ask R&D if they can combine several products into one. You are always better selling more of a few SKUs than a little of many SKUs. Yes, it's true.

Here is an example.

Leading container/closet company. We made the best wire closet systems. The problem was they were now too good. They would hold 20–50 percent more maximum weight than our fast-growing competition. Consumers, however, didn't need systems to hold that much weight anymore. Our plant was suffering, and the teams were out of ideas. We went back to R&D and asked them to re-spec the product. We found out they could reduce the size, weight, and number of rows in each shelf. They could also reduce the size of each metal rod. We could then simplify the manufacturing process. This changed most of the product specifications. This all took a lot of work…by R&D, marketing, manufacturing, sales, and finance. We relaunched. We got our business back and then some. The plant stayed open. Sales went up. R&D paid off.

These opportunities are everywhere. R&D teams are disciplined and project-focused. Can you say the same for sales? Marketing? All the time? Of course not.

Use your entire team to improve. That's the real hidden opportunity.

CHAPTER 46

Complex Plans Spell Certain Defeat

Incredible analysis, strategies, action plans, investments and policies can really help companies succeed. Usually well-known consulting groups, boards, successful CEOs, and others develop such documents and presentations.

Many times, these plans are very good, actually a marvel of activity, analysis, and strategies. The challenge, however, is these plans many times are too complex, time consuming, and costly. In addition, can the company employees understand and execute these new plans?

You may say, if the plans are too complex, get new people! (I have never seen that work—culture, industry knowledge, and performance are tied to approaches people can understand, with the time to execute.)

The results of complex business plans are usually all the same: defeat. Defeated employees, partners, and customers. In fact, things are usually worse than before such plans are (forced) upon the business.

Why? The reasons vary, but usually they are the following:

1. Lack of involvement and/or buy in by the business personnel.
2. The plans were not correct or not possible to execute (time, personnel, or resources).
3. The plans were not communicated correctly or often enough to all levels of the organization.

4. The reward structure was not aligned to the plans. (Don't be surprised here; this is a very common issue in most companies.)
5. The plans assume knowledge/talent in the organization that is not present...with no to little training.

What's a better approach? Pretty simple! First, don't do items 1–5 just outlined. Second, keep your plans simple. Great execution always beats great anything. Finally, consider this: If everyone can't understand your (complex) plans in a few pieces of paper or a one- to two-minute answer, try again.

We built a $5 billion company (from $3 billion) on one line: "Same (product) performance, less price."

So can you.

CHAPTER 47

The Chinese Restaurant Speed Model

Speed is a very compelling competitive advantage. It can separate you from the competition in so many ways. Used correctly, it can also provide increased sales, POS, and profits.

In Chapter 11, we talked a lot about SKU reduction, or the 80/20 approach to products. A principal benefit of the 80/20 is speed in development, manufacture, delivery, and sell-through. Let's look at a very successful example: takeout Chinese restaurants. They have large menus of many, many dishes and still deliver those dishes in ten to twenty minutes from order. Even fast-food drive-throughs with much smaller menus struggle to match the Chinese restaurant speed model.

How do they do it? What can you learn from them? How fast or efficient is your company? How about online orders? Mass merchant orders? Special orders?

Chinese restaurants are fast, efficient, and profitable because they really don't have fifty to seventy-five menu items. They really have around twenty. That's right. Why? Well, they have commonality of ingredients and mix and match them well in one packaging approach and offer takeout only (some now deliver). They operate in small footprints with just Chinese food.

Big menu, good prices. Speed. Great turnover. Low overhead.

You see, a Chinese restaurant's seventy-five or more offerings are really only a small "product line" of four proteins (beef, pork, fish, chicken), four to six vegetables, a few soups, a roll, two to three kinds of noodles, two portions of rice, two to three sauces, one cookie, two to three packaging containers, one bag, and one invoice. That's about twenty real product offerings.

Everything is mix and match. All precooked. Waiting. Brilliant.

Almost every business I have been part of benefits from such an approach. They say you can't teach speed in sports. It's true. You can, however, not only teach speed, but you can also master it in business.

Focus your product lines, use commonality of parts/ingredients, shorten supplier time lines, and help everyone focus on the 80/20 approach.

We did this in the bike business. We studied the Chinese restaurant. We then visited Asia and saw that model in place for bicycles. One big assembly factory and distribution center (together) but, more importantly, commonality of parts, paints, decals, and a supplier network required to be "on campus."

The US model had suppliers everywhere. Lead times were much longer. Changing SKUs took a long time, especially to meet fast-changing customer pricing demands.

We built two dedicated factories in North America (Mexico), focused on our two best Walmart sellers, and brought in suppliers on-site with extra inventory and decision makers. Our responsiveness (speed) tripled vs our old model.

We became the number one unit seller in the United States from our previous number four position. Speed kills (they say), in this case, our competition. In a seasonal business, we were also able to meet quick-changing POS and make all our deliveries on time.

"That fast enough for ya?" we asked. Sure was.

Still not as fast as those Chinese restaurants, though, so we kept at it. So can you!

CHAPTER 48

The Fireworks Lessons

Fireworks shows taught me a lot about human behavior (at work and in the community) and how to anticipate and manage such behavior. It's quite a story and learning. Everything from fireworks to police cars, fire departments, private jets, newspaper ads/stories, city council, CEOs, and lessons learned.

It started when I was in my first job in an ad/PR agency. I was twenty-four years old and somehow ended up managing the entertainment for three very large sales meetings in a mountain town for our largest client: an equipment company. Their new motorized equipment cost a lot, and our client had built a new plant to make them. It was now time to bring in hundreds of their dealers in three different meetings to see the plant and the new products and secure millions of dollars of orders. It was a time (especially compared to today) of a much more wide-open approach to business spending on sales and entertainment.

Believe it or not, my job (and support team) was to;

1. secure three golf courses for the three different dates for dealer tournaments;
2. secure twelve tennis courts for the same;
3. hire very well-known former or senior professional golfers and tennis players to attend these events with dealers (total of twelve athletes);

4. develop large, musical-based live motorized equipment "shows" at the plant;
5. stage themed multiple meals for the dealers, with entertainment;
6. secure the three largest and best hotels in town and book all the rooms;
7. coordinate all transportation;
8. develop with our client's company executives their dealer AV presentations (in those days, 35mm slides/projectors);
9. create photo-based memories for all dealers (the equipment show, pro athletes, tournaments, and the fireworks); and
10. create and present the biggest (surprise) fireworks shows ever in the town for the dealers…three times.

Let's focus on the fireworks shows. We located Rocky V (real name, sorta), a top fireworks show operation. Fireworks signs, mortars (yes, like in the war) and the new boomers (more about that later).

Turns out, we needed to basically rent the hotel's golf course's eighteenth fairway to build the fireworks battleground. Rocky's team dug areas for mortars. They constructed safe shooting zones. They also shipped enough fireworks for three fifteen- to twenty-minute "extravaganza" shows.

The fireworks shows cost a lot. The CEO of our client kept saying to do it top notch. (First lesson here: We should have gotten that order in writing. See Chapter 39.)

Our first dealer meeting went well. The fireworks show was good; the surprise worked, but it was not incredible according to our client. We had followed all the local rules for such a show (there were a lot). Still, we had a disappointed client. Did we misread the CEO? Yes. Did we/I probe enough? No. (Lesson 2: Ask. Make sure.)

So we upped our game. At the next meeting, there were more fireworks, some of the new boomers, and giant signs that fireworks lit up. The surprise worked again because the show was so much better and louder, more colorful, and well, an extravaganza!

The client was thrilled. The dealers were very impressed with everything. Millions and millions of business written. We were heroes! (Lesson 3: If you don't communicate well with all your audiences—in this case, the county board and another kind of "fireworks" can happen...)

I was back home between meetings—on a double date, in fact—basking in my glory. (Lesson 4: All glory is fleeting, especially when you don't anticipate well!) When somehow my father (no cell phones then) found me at my date's house, he told me the client, the director of marketing, called the house to find me. I needed to be at the airport at six o'clock the next morning. A private jet would be waiting to take me back to the site of the meetings/fireworks shows. Why? Dad wasn't told. End of date. What was going on?

The jet landed a bit before 9:00 a.m. Car waiting. The trade show manager, a good guy but a bit of a character, was waiting. He said, "We are going to the county courthouse for a hearing."

"Okay, but why do you need me?" I said.

He said, "Not sure. We will see."

Human behavior is pretty predictable. It's just when you are a young manager, you haven't learned that yet. You see, blame always travels downhill. (Lesson 5)

We arrived. We sat in the back row. It was probably twenty rows or so to the main table. Six county commissioners. Our main client was getting questioned about the fireworks show and why it was so loud versus the first show. They were not happy. They wanted the last (third) show cancelled. (We had all the fireworks bought, eighteenth fairway ready, and dealers coming to see the "bigger" surprise.)

The client pointed out to the county commissioners the company had made a big investment in the new plant and the dealer meetings, with huge spending in their town for the shows, and now, the company's new commitment to revise the fireworks show (*Really?* I thought). They told him about all the community calls questioning what the big noise was about (among other issues). Then it came. Our client said the company had chartered a private jet (kind of big deal back then) and had brought one of Chicago's top pyrotechnic experts to meet with the commissioners and make sure the last fireworks show would be done to their satisfaction.

What? Who the hell was that? I was the only guy on the jet that wasn't a pilot. Then our client announced the expert's name—mine! I was stunned. (Lesson 6: Get to meetings early!) Remember I said it was about twenty rows up to the commissioners' table. As I walked up to the table, I had that much time to become a pyrotechnic expert! As I walked by my client, he turned around facing me and said, "Let's see what $50 an hour can do" (that was a big billing rate back then).

Needless to say, they thought I was very young to be such an expert. First of all, I clarified I had managed other fireworks shows (true) but was not certified PE, but I did know enough to answer their questions. They asked me about sound levels, height of fireworks displays, timing, and a community attendee plan. That plan said we had to invite all local residents, with full page ads in the local newspapers, to the event (it was supposed to be a surprise, so they agreed the community could watch from the shopping center below the hotel). We also had to hire their town's off-duty sheriffs (handle crowd control) and the firemen (to "help" our fireworks team!). We agreed. We got back to the hotel. The CEO said the whole incident was my agency's fault (we all knew it was really the CEO's but…) So he then decided not only were we *not* going to tone down the show, especially since it was the last show, but we were also going to "up" the boomers big time. He wasn't going to "let anyone tell him what to do." (His language was more colorful…)

(Lesson 7: Get your supervisor involved, which I did but too late, it turned out.) We then did everything required by the commission, except the boomers, that were hard to control completely. A big community crowd came to see the fireworks. The dealers were excited to see the biggest show ever! The sheriff and fire departments were there, getting paid with the police who were at the shopping center. Let the show begin.

It sounded like WWIII. The boomers actually cracked walls in the hotel. The mortars fired and fired. There was so much smoke from the eighteenth fairway you couldn't see it. The sky was alive with color and sound. The client was ecstatic.

It was then our client contact noticed police cars coming up to the hotel. Seems they wanted to talk to the fireworks people. The client. The agency coordinator. Everyone.

Remember I said problems roll downhill? The CEO and VP clients claimed they didn't direct the bigger, louder show. (Not true!) The fireworks guys said they just did what they were hired to do. The agency team (us) were told we should (must) leave (now) by the client (the marketing director, who said he would "handle it"). All glory (again) dashed. (Lesson 8: Beware of the possible consequences of your actions, regardless of the client's, boss's, or customer's wishes, as if there's an issue, can you trust them?)

The rest remains a mystery to this day. We left that night. We believe the issues were settled between the client and the county.

So when you want to be the big-time fireworks person, make sure you (or others) don't bring those fireworks down on you!

CHAPTER 49

New Blood: Interns

What a great opportunity for everyone—interns!

New blood! New ideas. Enthusiasm. Energy. Open-mindedness. Ready to learn. No "bad" habits. No predetermined decisions. No "that won't work."

Little experience, yes, but the latest learnings and some of college's brightest future stars are now working for you. Plus, they will know your company if you later hire them.

We would always hire as many interns as we could. Over 30 percent came to work for us after graduation. No recruiting. No fees. Ready to go.

My experiences with intern programs were good every time, every year, every company.

Here are some things we learned:

1. Yes, you will get numerous requests from employees, suppliers, customers, and others to hire "their kid" as an intern. This is okay as long as they are qualified and earn the job in the interview process.
2. Consider interns from all schools, not just the top-rated institutions. Why? We found a diverse group produced more effective interns. In addition, interns from less-known schools always seemed to perform better as interns—they had more to prove, it turned out.

3. Pay your interns. It creates a real-life situation and incentivizes them to do their best work...all the time.
4. Release interns who don't perform, are disruptive, or are not on time. Yep. You are not a babysitting service. Life lesson number 1 for interns.
5. Use your interns. Give them a lot to do. Be creative. It works!

So there you go! Get some "new blood"!

CHAPTER 50

The Local Advantage

"There's no place like home."

Throughout my career, I learned this lesson over and over. You want to understand and succeed in an international market? Hire a local manager or distributor. You want to sell more into any key region, market, or to a specialty customer? Hire a local. You want faster service? Hire the local supplier. You want to lead a region or country sales team or even be a successful CEO? Go local.

Why is local better? You intuitively know. Locals know the culture, rules, people, and most importantly, what works and what doesn't. They know how to get things done. You see, you may develop and launch a great product, sales plan, and distribution approach and never understand why it didn't work. You, most likely, didn't know what you didn't know. You also were probably not in the market or with the local team. The classic mistake most US companies make—or any company for that matter—is putting home office/country personnel into leadership positions in foreign countries. Rarely have I seen this be successful. The gap of understanding from language, customs, relationships, and trust are just too challenging. Yes, we supposedly live in a global business world. How are home office personnel supposed to learn? My answer was always the same: at someone else's company!

This is also true for the "commuter" leader. Such leaders send a very clear message: Living with the local team and in the market is not important enough to move there. Thus, the local people, suppliers, and customers find it hard to commit to such a leader. In addition, the commuter leader never really learns what they need to know about the company's people, culture, or market(s). In fact, it's why when I was president and/or CEO, it was required (if you worked for us) to live in the market or assigned office. Period.

Did we lose some people? We did. Did, in every case (six companies), we succeed and do better with the local leader than the team before us (with a commuter)? Every time.

Teams work well together when they are together. In each case, after my team left each of these six companies—and all of them then allowed many commuter leaders—they saw financial performance decline, usually by more than 20 percent. Like this book says, "It's impossible to commit to maybe." That's what the local commuters want the people to do: commit to the non-committed leader. Flat out, that just doesn't work out very well and costs the company much more than the hire is worth.

So how do you find and capitalize on the "local advantage"?

1. *Do your homework.* Find the best local sales leaders for your international regions.
2. *Build a culture of commitment.* Get your team to live in the right place. Use rewards, housing, incentives, and career path opportunities but get everyone together.
3. *Do not make exceptions.* Do not fall for the "intention" to move promise. Be understanding of family needs, but if they cannot move within ninety days, select a different candidate. In my experience, only 15 percent of current company managers will move. So actively recruit…all the time. It's a lot more effective and less costly (versus declining performance) than the commuter leader.
4. *Find the local suppliers.* Require your team (or yourself) to partner with and assist key local providers. Here's an example. In the bike business, the Asian plants/companies required all their suppliers to be on site at their plant with trained personnel, equipment, and supplies. Why? It made them faster. It also helped them to be the lower cost

supplier (and their teams could react in person on a daily basis.) The other model—mostly a US one—was suppliers all over the globe. That appeared to be less costly. Usually, it wasn't. That model was slower, had a lot of delays, and had a very challenging supply and communications issues. We proved it in the bike business. We went local. We built bikes in North America, using the Asian model. We won, beating the US and Asian companies. How? Speed. You can achieve this as well. (See Chapter 47.)

5. *Be better prepared for when the storms come.* Business is full of challenges. When they come, local suppliers, personnel, and leadership will be in a much better position to react quicker and more successfully because there they are together. They know the culture, marketing, and how to get things done. Here's an example: Our largest customer needed an emergency alkaline batteries order and a packaging change…all in one week. It was worth $10 million and a placement for the holidays of $35 million more. Our Asian plant (which we were closing) could not do it. Our local plant (scheduled to be closed by previous management) could. We got the order and delivered. We went on to double the business. How? "The local advantage."

THE MANAGEMENT
POLITICS GAME

CHAPTER 51

You Can't Do Better Than "Yes"

How many times have you worked hard to get something approved, and while talking to a board member, your manager, even outside work, a banker, or in your personal life, you present your case and the person says *yes*?

Right there, you have gotten what you were after. Walk away. Stop talking. Quit rationalizing. Don't tell them how smart they are. Don't keep explaining why they are so smart to have said yes—you have already gotten your answer. You see, you can't do better than yes.

You would not believe how many people—once they have a yes—continue to talk, continue to present, continue to go on and on…until at some point, the person who is giving you the yes starts to doubt their decision. They think, *Why are they trying so hard?* And things can then get reversed!

I'll give you a perfect example. When I was a very young man working in an agency, I was with a *very* well-known pro tennis great. We were sitting in Palm Springs, California, at a bar. My assignment was to try to convince him to endorse a tennis racquet again late in his career and doing a whole media tour, knowing he did really not have to do this.

I presented my case with a lot of passion and excitement, and he sat there and listened attentively, sipping a drink. I continued to present and present, and he finally said, "Yes, I'll do it." I was so thrilled I continued to tell him what a good idea it was, all the things we were going to do, and why he was going to be happy with this idea.

He continued to listen attentively, and then finally, he stopped, put his hand on mine, and said, "Dave, you can't do better than *yes*."

Simple. Thank you. Stopped discussing it. Got started on that yes!

CHAPTER 52

But We Are Afraid of "Jackie"!

We have talked a lot about careers and how to move forward. But careers also have a big impact on your personal life and family. Some people are comfortable with moving several times; others rationalize they can't do this to their kids or spouse. They need to stay in one place, at one school, and grow up there. I'm not sure there's any real data to prove what's better either way.

In my case, I did move my kids a lot. They did experience a lot. I thought it helped them grow up, see different areas and experience different people. But it was hard. Just like when you join a new company, it's the same for your family (new doctors, schools, friends, cultures, etc.). Still, it can be invigorating! So how do you help manage this? The first step is to get the parents to sit down with their kids, explain the situation, and then tell the truth to the employer who has asked them to move.

But what about the chapter headline, "But We Are Afraid of Jackie"? I had a CFO who had lived in the southeast, and we had tried everything to get him to move to our new headquarters. First, he said his wife didn't want to move. Then he didn't want to move. Then his kids didn't want to move.

We finally got it down to one of his three daughters—a teenager who had a boyfriend at their local high school. They just didn't know how to talk to her about it, and when they did, she got very upset to the point they admitted later they were afraid of her emotions and didn't know how to deal with them. So at times, we may all be afraid of "Jackie."

A lot of parents are that way. But one thing I learned as a young father was from my father. He said, "You know, a parent's job is to prepare your children to become adults. They have friends. They don't really know what moving will be like. Some will handle it well and some won't."

Present your case. Go show them the school, the city. Have them meet some local kids. Think about what's the best in the long term for them and for you and your family. Put all the facts on the table. After you have done all this, the answer should be clear. And don't be afraid of "Jackie."

PS They did move. She didn't miss the boyfriend after three weeks. The CFO made bundles of cash and never regretted the move. (See Page 215)

CHAPTER 53

Your Dad Called

Three words that strike fear in most people! You can also have a similar feeling when you get the message that the chairman of the board called, your boss called, your number one customer called, or one of your kids called.

Running a business leaves you open to a lot of potential surprises. Just like when you get the message your dad called. Usually that call is about one of three things: someone died, you need to pay back the money you borrowed, or he needs you to call your mother! Business calls can be very similar when you're not ready. Maybe you were hoping that the problems would just go away and no one would really call you on them!

But the calls always come, and if you're not prepared, they usually do not go well, so what's the lesson here? You should be calling them before they call you. Don't avoid problems or confrontations or difficult situations; they usually just get worse. It also says something about you as a manager or leader. Get the facts, prepare, and then be proactive, and this will allow you to manage the situation and to run the business the way it should be run. You can practice on these calls with your dad, mom, or kids. The result? No more "Your dad called" messages!

CHAPTER 54

Electronic Bullies

Work is over. It's late. It's not long after you discussed this subject. Then it comes, like out of the blue. An email, voice message, text, even a faxed note. An attack. An unfair, usually stab-you-in-the-back message. A rant. A threat. An unbelievable, BS request, order, comment, or God knows what.

Such things ever happen to you? Of course! Why? You know why. From whom? From the electronic bully! Someone who is a non-professional person who can only hide behind their phone, computer, or whatever thing they can because they are the electronic bully.

The real question is (once your anger subsides), what are you gonna do about it? Respond quickly? Attack back? Try to understand why this is happening, and professionally ask them? All understandable responses. Still, will it stop the electronic bully? Probably not-ever.

So what to do?

Usually this is your superior or someone who thinks they are. Sometimes it's someone competing with you, a rival. So here are some approaches that have worked for me:

1. Do not respond until you can see that person. Then confront them directly, professionally, and with facts. Backstop this approach by confiding in a trusted HR person or work associate who is also involved. Why? Two "same" stories

are better than one, especially if it blows up. Know this: The electronic bully will do everything possible to avoid this meeting and demand you answer electronically. Don't do it.

2. If you cannot do number 1, simply say you do not know and you will get back to them. Then you go find them and do number 1!

3. If impossible to meet on Facetime, write a well-thought-out response and copy their boss, your boss, and anyone else relevant. Kaboom! This approach is number 3 because you tried number 1 and number 2! You say this is risky. So is being bullied.

In time, the electronic bully will move on, or you will.

It's an unfortunate consequence of today's electronic world, the age of the electronic bully. The best approach is head on.

Go in person. Facetime. Talk on the phone. It's your best chance to be successful. Unplug that bully!

CHAPTER 55

A Castle Cannot Hold Two Kings

An executive in Scandinavia told me this about castles and kings. He told me it's an old saying (truth). It's a lot like "a boat has just one captain." The message is the same. Presidents, GMs, CEOs, board members, COBs, executive COBs, and every manager in business at every level knows what works best—one person in charge of their function. Yes, matrix organizations, non-profit boards, unions, etc., all try to have multiple or co-leaders. How about co-CEOs? Talk about confusion! There is only one pairing of power that I have seen work: That's Mom and Dad. Still, notice I said *Mom* first!

While you may think we do have clear titles and responsibilities in today's business organizations (save the dreaded matrix approach), it's the overreaching investors, board members, chairman, and former leaders who continue to create the chaos in today's companies.

Straight up, I believe it's the increasing amount of investor/board/chairman on today's boards who believe they know better than the operators on how to run the company that are really hurting businesses. It's really their short-term financial engineering they insist on that does it. The two groups are headed in opposite directions. Underperformance is the result, if not worse.

So who's in charge? Who do the people listen to? Leadership confusion undermines the very essence of what is needed to succeed. This, added to the stock buy-back strategy of PE/hedge fund investors pushed on companies, even further weakens the company (versus R&D, capital investments, employee rewards). I see, if you have no ideas on how to groom/fix a company, then all you can do is buy back the stock for those investors who will leave the minute they can. Yes, maybe the CEO gets rich too…maybe. What is left, though?

Along the way, the castle crumbles. The boat goes off course. Two kings, captains, or leaders all send the same message: We don't agree or know what to do.

So then what do you do?

It depends on the scope of the issues. If you're a manager, division president, or GM, find a way to reorganize and get clear lines of authority, even if you have to give up some functions. Success is dependent on clear lines of responsibility and direction. Organization and compensation drive behavior. Period.

If you're in the board room, especially a CEO, you can approach it several ways. Here's some that worked for me:

1. Find something else for the other wannabe king to do. Like help lead key board committees or M&A or tasks with analysts. Keep them busy and involved but away from operations. They will never understand until they are actually responsible for operations, in the meantime they will negatively affect operations.

2. Get the "two kings" thing changed. The other king will stay at it until you give in, meaning you will fail, rarely make money, and be unproductive. Yes, you can try to talk it out with other king, but it rarely changes. Usually a top-to-top with the aspiring king's superiors will work.

3. Finally, get the aspiring king removed from board. Build consensus among the board, larger investors, and/or management. Be prepared to leave, and even negotiate a package (that you like) with those responsible before you make your play. Hoping it will get better is not a strategy!

It's not a good situation, but it always ends the same: one castle, one king.

CHAPTER 56

Results Are the Real Power

Who really has the power in business? The power to decide, to impact your team? You or owners? Board of directors? CEOs? Customers? Your boss? They do. They have "granted" power.

How do you achieve power? Born into the job? Politics? Friendships? Financial investment? Perhaps, but it will be fleeting.

The only power worth having, I have found, is through consistent, positive results. Financial, of course, but also in leadership, relationships, vision, actions, and very importantly, building trust.

Such power enables you to build teams and strategic plans (see Chapter 31, "The Five Steps") and execute them without all the other political, ownership, and financial issues derailing those plans.

Make and exceed your financial commitments. Be the consistent, trusted leader who has the entire team and company in mind. Develop and execute the vision and strategy without diverting for political or short-term financial issues (see Chapter 1, "Stay in Formation").

Success has many parents, failure none. Either way, you will be challenged to change too quickly and revise promises, strategies, and even compensation programs. Get good results, and keep these other non-productive issues at the door.

You say, "How do you get good results all the time?"

Read this book! Ha ha. Really, you do your job the right way. Most good to great CEOs to managers know how to be successful. The question is at what? Politics first? Then the job?

Job first. Good results. Politics are for non-performers and are not needed. Everybody wants to win. The question is, "In what manner?" Everybody also knows you can't trust the politician, the greedy one, or the non-committed (see Chapter 3, "It's Impossible").

This is a critical decision in your career. Who are you gonna be? The shortcut politician? Or the trusted leader, one that is on a more difficult path but, in the long run, more rewarding?

So go get great results. Your power will be earned. You will never have to be that politician.

It's the real power. One that lasts.

CHAPTER 57

Working Remotely: A Lot to Consider

Sometimes dreams do come true. Or do they?

In 2020, a global pandemic created the need for most employees to work remotely. Video conferencing, phone calls, texts, mail, and faxes became the primary communication model.

So did working from one's home. Another big shift happened as well. Many employees reevaluated their career choice, current job, commute and the home versus office work experience.

Companies, faced with numerous challenges—especially employee health and work restrictions—had to adapt to the ever-changing situations. Employees, faced with new challenges, sought out working remotely and had direct experience doing it. It has and will continue to impact employment choices, locations, and personal communications.

So if you have transitioned to working remotely, is it working out? Do you think you would like to do it permanently? Why? Why not? Are you trying to decide whether or not to pursue remote-only jobs? Clearly, there are several jobs well suited for working remotely. There are also many personal reasons for doing the same.

After I retired, I myself worked remotely on several boards and projects. I also have spent a lot of time talking to many employees, management teams, and other leaders about working remotely versus in person. While there are many issues, the ones we focused on the most were the longer-term issues of working exclusively remotely. Let's review several of these topics on a personal basis:

1. Does your desire to work remotely overcome your needs for in-person communication?
2. Do you believe your absence in the office or not meeting with customers or suppliers in person will impact your effectiveness due to communicating remotely versus in person?
3. Do you think your career advancement will be impacted by exclusively working remotely?

Working remotely is a bit like the commuter manager—those don't live near the office or area they are responsible. The difference here is the manager, at times, does go into the office and sees customers or suppliers and other employees in person. My experiences universally showed the commuter manager was not as effective, especially as a leader, as the in-person manager (see chapter 37).

Still, the opportunity to work remotely is an evolving change in the workplace, one much more personal than most. It is also one to explore, test, and review on an ongoing basis. As with most choices in one's career, there are pros and cons.

In the end, it appears that those jobs where in-person communications are key, especially for very career-orientated individuals, working remotely will be more challenging. To those where personal needs are more key, working remotely may be the answer, at least for periods of time.

In my career and after a lot of input from other managers, working and doing business in person (whenever possible) will most likely be the most effective way to communicate and, in turn, advance one's career. The good news is that it appears you will be able to test all approaches!

Everyone's dream is different. Follow yours!

CHAPTER 58

How to Make Your Bonus

You already know a lot of people do not "make" their bonus, fewer exceed the 100 percent payout, and almost no one makes their bonus regularly.

Why?

Well, targets are usually based on "sales prevention" (as in let's hold sales until next year), stretched goal numbers, or multiple unreasonable and/or not understood targets. Other times, targets are tilted to certain groups (especially corporate groups), with higher goals for operating divisions.

In addition, many employees have little input in the development of their bonus goals, their makeup, or the ever-increasing complexity of the programs (as in it's very difficult to track progress.)

Now you say this is a pretty negative view. Yes, it is. That's because it's one of most political, emotional, and complicated (unfortunately) programs in employee compensation and engagement.

It's my view effective bonus programs need to be very performance driven, with highly motivating targets designed to encourage employee behaviors the company feels will propel its employees to reach and exceed the key financial goals.

So what can you do to make your bonus in this environment? First, understand the process: Senior management usually relies on consultants, to compile "industry data," competitive data, and regional and national data. It looks at the company's bonus program's past results (payout versus goals, company financial performance).

Ownership and the BOD also has its perceptions (usually very political) and input (and ultimate approval). Investors also put demands on the company for what it spends, especially bonuses and stock awards. This is a lot of activity, you say. Sure is. Ad budgets, D&T budgets, even COGS get approved much easier and quicker. Why? People love to know what (other) people make. They want to be involved. It's all here, almost every human emotion but especially greed. Can "they" get better performance from employees without paying more?

It's been my experience all this activity (how to limit bonuses) severely holds back company performance on many levels. (See Chapter 8: "Compensation and Organization Drive Behavior")

Still, let's focus on how you can make your bonus. Let's look at a ten-step plan to bonus achievement:

1. Understand the process.
2. Get involved in any way you can in that process.
3. Develop your ideas and plans that have worked (previously or elsewhere), and match them to company goals/needs.
4. Get with others and your supervisor/mentor(s), and get their input. Refine your plan ideas.
5. Arrange to get these ideas and targets to your supervisor and your HR representative.
6. Assemble your facts to help develop what you believe the appropriate targets are.
7. Negotiate with all concerned; outline what you believe is fair to the company and yourself. This is the most important step. The best chance to get what you want is to negotiate.
8. Realize some targets you cannot directly affect. Still, tell your story!
9. Know that simple, easy-to-understand, and less complex programs *always* work better. Again, negotiate. Get facts to prove your points.
10. Finally, position yourself to focus on the plan. Understand what to spend your time on to maximize your achievements versus the targets.

Drive yourself to relentless pursuit of your targets. Do not waste time and effort on any other things that are not rewarded. It is the company's job to develop effective compensation programs. This is the plan now, so work it. Focus on the results needed to make that bonus. Remind everyone about the same thing. Teams make bonuses, driven by focused leaders. Go!

This is how to make your bonus...every year. Oh yeah!

That's the Same as Selling 100,000 Toasters!

One of the companies (actually a division) we ran sold kitchen appliances, including toasters. This division was part of a merger we had done to help us financially and our majority investor.

After the process, we needed to hire multiple bankers to raise funds for the corporation. Most employees don't realize how expensive such "raises" are, many times exceeding millions of dollars in fees. This particular one included one of the bank groups from our purchase. They would now be part of the "raise" offering group and be paid for such work.

We didn't feel we needed them, but still, they were friends of ownership, so they got paid...a lot.

We joked all they did was carry offering books around during our pitches.

It made the "raise" net proceeds less than planned and less than we had targeted.

The lesson here is twofold:

1. Favors' payback is very expensive. Be careful.
2. Such extra costs unnecessarily restrict companies' abilities to compete, invest, and build businesses.

You see, in this case, that extra cost literally cost all the margin we made on selling one hundred thousand toasters!

It's just a different way at looking at financial engineering and its true, real costs. You could say we were "toasted."

CHAPTER 60

The Night of the Generals

They say you don't want to get caught between a "rock and a hard place." How about between a "bullet and a target?"

Politics. Egos. Power. Anger. These traps are all there just waiting for their victims. Whether you are in a good place with the leaders of your organization or not, you must be careful not to insert yourself into their world, one you have no idea of what is (really) going on and why.

As a young VP at a key trade show, I did just that—inserted myself into their first in-person meeting. A walkaround, which included my superior, the president, his president of North America (possible replacement), the new chairman of the board, and the new CEO of our acquiring company from Scandinavia. Four generals overseeing a company that only needed two. This "Night of the Generals" was their first time all together. It was tense. Who would survive? Who would rise up to make the key decisions? Who liked whom? Who trusted whom? Was there already a (secret) plan? (Yes, of course—we just got acquired!)

So instead of staying out of the fray, I jumped right in. It was technically "my" businesses' trade show, so I figured I would get to know the new guys, impress them, and be so, so smart.

Well, unlike the "smart" cavalry leader who always sent a scout down the (potential) valley of death first, I proceeded with no preparation and little feel for the politics, the situation, or what was really going on. No scouting done.

Learning the hard way is just that, a hard lesson.

It didn't take two minutes before not only did it create a firestorm, but I was also told to leave by my superior immediately. He also let me know I needed to learn what I was saying before I said something so embarrassing it made me look unprepared and unprofessional. This said in front of all four "generals."

He was right. In a tense, political, "unscouted" situation, I accomplished the exact opposite impression I wanted.

What was it I said? Just this: I decided "I" would introduce them to each other and, in doing so, got most of their official titles wrong. *Bam!*

That was it. The perfect tension explosion. My boss had to correct me and get the titles correct.

Later, the president, a really great leader, stopped by my room to explain and even (sorta) apologize for jumping on me. Still, my comments went to the core of their emotions, tensions, and political issues. Everyone was now in a bad place.

What was to be learned here? I was told;

1. Get my facts right, all of them, before approaching senior management/BOD/superiors.
2. Do not insert yourself into your leader(s) issues, especially when they are together unless absolutely necessary (like almost never).
3. Most heroes die. Jumping into your "general's" world to impress, save the company, or save them is just like stepping between a "bullet and target."

What happened? The acquiring CEO removed my boss and the chairman of the board. I survived…barely. From then on, I always sent a scout first!

Your Life Team: Mentors, Parents, and Spouses

How do we learn to be successful?

Education? Experience? Breaks? Training? Yep. How else?

By asking questions then listening. Accept there are those who know you well and have a perspective you may not. They can help you think differently. Help you to travel down the "road less traveled."

In my case, I was lucky to have several impactful business mentors, two very supportive but direct parents, and a much smarter, less emotional, and keenly observant spouse. We all may feel others usually "don't understand" our situation and dismiss their comments and/or help. Mistake. When you are in trouble or are in a tough situation, you have already waited too long. Check in regularly with your "life team." You say you haven't formed it yet. No need. They are all right there. Just ask.

I can say without my life team, there is little chance I would have achieved what I did in business…and life.

Here's a few examples:

1. *Mentor 1.* President of the golf company where I worked. He took the time to help turn a thirty-ish VP into a much better leader. I was then a poor listener, a one-dimensional, judgmental driver for results. Few trust or want to follow such a leader.

He showed me how listening first works so much better (what's on their list?). Not only do you now know what's important to them, but you can also revise your approach and requests/directions. He taught me about building teams (see Chapter 28). He stepped me through the Barbell approach (see Chapter 20) business strategy. He made me develop five-point plans (see Chapter 31) over and over.

His (and my spouse's) greatest compliment about me was "You have the capability to learn and are resilient. Use those traits, and things will work out."

It took a while, but embracing learning enabled life-long success. It never stops. Seek it out. Let it in. Listen. Recover. Revise. React.

2. *Mentor 2.* He was a Jesuit priest. He was also a counselor I went (kind of forced!) to see when I was going through a major and dramatic life change.

It was in these meetings, in humble surroundings, with a quiet, sincere man (whom I felt I was so much stronger than he…at first), I learned about "inner strength."

It was painful, long, upsetting, and time consuming. (You say you don't need counseling. Maybe not, but that's not the point here.) His "inner strength" and conviction was that of Hercules. He saw that I did things others did not ask me to do or say and then wanted credit for it. When that didn't happen, I got upset, even resentful.

He put it plainly: "If you send things/thoughts/actions across the river in your boat, even though those people did not ask you for it, do not get upset if the boat doesn't come back to you full of thanks. It was you who decided such an action, not them." The learning here was to be true to yourself. Do things that help you learn. Fixing others or looking for unrequested thanks isn't learning; it's self-adoration. Your life team can help you improve your management style and learning more than you know.

3. *Parents*. Usually a good relationship here helps you your entire life. If there are no parents or they chose not to help, okay. You will find others to play those roles (siblings, friends).

    Still, parents/family have unique insights into your personality, how you "roll," and your impact on others.

    My dad, a lifetime AT&T manager, was rooted in sales and believed results speak for themselves. He also knew people you trusted were the ones to depend on. One story about this is a "Beware of what you want" lesson. As a VP at the sporting goods company, I went to the president and asked for a chance to move from the top marketing/ad job to a line position (VP footwear/clothing/licensing).

    Well, the president listened and said okay! (I was thrilled, sitting in first class with him flying to a trade show.) Then he said he didn't need me in "that" job but did need a VP he could trust (there's that word again. See Chapter 63) in the top sales position in the golf division. Why? He had trust issues with the current golf division president. He also said he would watch over me and make sure nothing "unusual" happened. I was floored. Sales? Really? Up to that point I had no experience in sales. The golf president was also someone I did not trust or want to work for—the request had backfired!

    The company president told me to let him know on Monday morning if I would accept the job. I got home, called my parents, and said when we came down for Sunday dinner, I had something to talk to them about. Long story short. After two hours explaining things at the parents' house and all my reasons why I couldn't take the sales job and I should pass on the offer, my dad had said very little on the whole situation. So I called him out. I asked why and asked what he thought. Again, a life team member would cut right through it (and me). He said the following:
    - "You said this is what you want, to go into a line position?" (Yes.)

- "The president of the company gives you that opportunity, a little different job but it was best for the company?" (Well, yes.)
- "He also said he would take care of you in this position because he needs someone he can trust?" (Yes.)
- "Okay, I (Dad) am going to bed." (What?)

It took me about ten minutes to get it. Dad saw it was what I "needed" to do, that I could do it, and it was just different from what I had thought.

He later said, "You got what you asked for. That's the best you can do!"

On Monday, I took the job. It was the single most important step in my career. It got me "into the real game."

Probably would never have happened without the life team.

4. *Spouse.* She has her master's degree in advertising. She worked in Chicago for two of the top ad agencies. She married me after four years (another story) of dating. We are a great pair. Totally different but so much alike on the important things. She avoids confrontations, drama, emotion, and being judgmental. I do not.

Throughout my career, I, at times, have shared with her my frustrations, challenges, and people issues. She listened attentively. She seldom gave much feedback unless asked. It routinely gave me another perspective I didn't have...or want to consider!

Many times in my career, I have felt I was right and needed to get that across to senior management and/or the board. Several times, especially later in my career, it worked. Two of the first three times, however, it did not work. The result was I left those companies. After the second time, she invited me out on a boat in Colorado (I love boating). The lake water temp was 38 degrees (no swimming to shore!) She said we needed to talk about my career.

This "help" was straightforward. She said, "If you want to still run companies, you need to learn to work with the owners/board/senior managers, not against them. That is how it works."

I was stunned. I began the rebuttal. She stopped me. "We are not moving the kids again because you always have to be right. I married you because you are a good learner. Time to do that."

That was it. I changed (best I could). It worked.

Life teams. Life awareness. Life changing. For life.

Tell the Truth

Telling the truth several times in my career cost me jobs, promotions, friends, and opportunities. You see, most people "can't handle the truth." (Yes, Jack Nicholson, *A Few Good Men*). They just want to hear the "best case." Still, overall in my career, telling the truth worked out pretty well! The truth provides the key information business people need to know to be successful long term. The truth about the why, where, when, and how things happened and can be improved is the ticket.

Now many people (managers, interviewers) hide certain information until later. Many don't want to "face the music" just yet, a bit afraid to tell the whole story. Seems like the accepted approach, doesn't it? It might even work for a while. It may buy you time. It may get you the job. The problem is you haven't properly set the situation up on an honest and truthful basis. You have no room to go back and reset it without losing considerable confidence of those you didn't tell the truth to in the first place. That's trust (see Chapter 63). You get just one chance. Even though the 2000s introduced us all to fake news, false claims, and overpromising, it doesn't mean it will work long term in business. You see, business, unlike politics, has a real scorecard for all to see.

In several chapters in the book, I outline several lessons learned about trust, honesty, and how to succeed in challenging situations. Here are some lessons I learned about telling the truth directly:

1. *The bike business/division of a large corporation.* When I took the job, I had two choices in the first week: support the group president and his skewed assessment (we were doing much better than we were, and things were turning around) or tell the unadulterated truth (just the opposite of his story). You speculate, was I just trying to set things up better for myself? True, to a point. But, by his sugar coating the division's performance it meant all the bike employees had no chance at fixing the business because the capital funds we would need would be gone in the annual plan. The CEO would also tell a much better story to the board and Wall Street. It would then later all come crashing down on everyone. The CEO who hired me had a few rules to live by. He outlined them at our first meeting:
   - Tell the truth.
   - Do what you say, when you say.
   - Lead by example.

   So that's exactly what I did. It wasn't pretty. It was very difficult. I didn't work for the group president anymore. And we tripled the sales and profits of the division versus shutting it down. No apologies to the board or Wall Street. The truth rebuilt the business. Everyone won…except that group president.

2. *Large consumer storage business/division of a large corporation.* The CEO of the corporation launched a bold strategy for this business before I was hired. Trouble was, it backfired. The business, whose COGS were over 65 percent based on plastic (oil), had skyrocketed. The reduced customer pricing designed to gain share now moved the product margins to negative (as in less than zero), and the large, new manufacturing plants were half-full (with large negative plant variances). The task now was to deal with these issues and

get the CEO and board (who had approved the now very costly strategy) to acknowledge the situation and then follow through on the turnaround plan.

Again, we followed the "Tell the Truth" playbook. This time, though, it was via one-on-one meetings with the corporation's COO, CFO, and CEO. When you follow the truth strategy, it's also a very good idea to have a plan on how to fix the problems! We did. We closed the new plants, raised prices (a lot), exited hundreds of millions of dollars of business, and used the 80/20 approach for remaining products. (See Chapter 11)

It worked but only because the whole truth was told, enabling us to move quickly, boldly, and without internal political risk. The team before us, the sorta truth guys, lost millions and thousands of jobs. We turned that $60M loss to $15M EBIT. Truth is the difference so many times. That and courage.

3. *The lost CEO job.* Later in my career, I had a great job and team. Unfortunately, there were some issues I was uncomfortable about and explored options. I then got an opportunity to become the CEO of another very large company that I felt good about. I became the lead outside candidate and had my final interview with the board. They asked me about their situation. I told them the truth: I would, if things continued as they were, sell two divisions and agree to stay the three years it would take to complete the job. I would also commit to train their internal candidate (whom they said was not ready yet to be CEO). A few board members pressed me on my strategy (they hoped, somehow, things would turn around without selling the division[s]). They were, however, retiring their current CEO with that very strategy. They wanted me to stay at least five years. Again, I told the truth. I stayed with my strategy. We decided not to go forward. They hired the internal guy. The new CEO, in a top-to-top customer meeting six months later hosted by a common, top retailer, not knowing it was me who was

almost his boss, asked me and the other participating CEO there what he should do about his situation with his company and the retailer since this was his first time as CEO. We told him what we thought. The truth.

PS About a year later, they "had to" sell those divisions. I finished my career at my current company…in a better financial situation.

Why You Fire Those Who Don't Trust

What is trust? Where you put your money? Can be. It's also one of the most important beliefs in business, relationships, and life.

Trust usually has to be earned over time. Yes, some people appear trustworthy in your first meeting. Others absolutely do not and may never. In most cases, you won't really know if you can trust someone for a while if you are lucky. Sometimes you will never know. Trust is elusive and can change. Trust is, however, the key to successful relationships and, in turn, business success.

There are examples of businesses succeeding despite the lack of trust, but sooner or later, that will break down with negative results.

How do you determine trustworthiness? This is a tough one. Let's step back and review those people, businesses, or organizations you do trust. Is it any of the following?

- Your experience with them
- Specific times they were there for you
- Do they consistently tell the truth? Are they honest?
- Do they do what they say when they say?
- Is it a feeling?
- Can you sense it?
- Do you believe in them?

That's a good list. How about because, time and time again, they have proved it and have earned your trust?

You can depend on them. They can depend on you. You both win. It's a two-way street.

You feel comfortable recommending them to others.

You have no hesitation in working with or for them or them working for you. You trust them to do the right thing. There is little to no envy, politics, or risks. They won't steal your money, job, or friends.

This is exactly why, sooner or later, those people or suppliers you don't trust, you will fire or get them fired.

Otherwise, they will do to you and/or your business one or many of the things people who haven't earned your trust do: poison you and/or your business.

The other person you will learn not to trust is the "overpromiser" (OP), as in committing things (usually compensation or title/jobs) to you in return for your agreement and/or actions.

This happens at all levels. The OP usually lacks the power, confidence, or their supervisor's/board approval to commit things to you but have learned it is the only way (they) can get people to follow them.

The worst case of overpromising, time and time again, was when I was a leader at a growing company. My OP's violated that most sacred promise, that being after I promised my staff what they committed to if we reached certain goals.

We beat our goals. Things didn't work out as promised.

We, as a group, "fired" them in so many ways. You cannot depend on a lie, a "maybe" or "I tricked you" (you lose). Never trust the OP as OPs don't trust themselves.

That old saying, "One rotten apple spoils the entire batch," is true. Trust me.

CHAPTER 64

The Blame Game

Business managers (all levels, types, and friends and foes) have made an art of the Blame Game. You see, it's always someone else's fault things are not going well or have gone badly.

In almost every situation, blame is assigned to the previous manager or team, both quickly and usually without a lot of facts. The other thing is this blame is why the current manager and/or team is not responsible for the current issues. In this situation, the question is, when is the current manager or team responsible for the results?

In my experience, this time of responsibility should be no more than twelve months. In reality, based on the politics involved, it can go on for two, even three, years. Why? Some managers are very good at politics. Others are good at pulling in all the previous decision makers and putting them in the position to protect this manager/team in order to protect themselves.

The problem with the Blame Game is it usually paralyzes the organization and things do not get better. (When everyone has a "get out of jail free" card, it's hard to improve things.)

Now let's assume you have inherited the bad situation. You know it was not your fault (maybe others do or don't). How do you handle the Blame Game correctly?

Here are some proven approaches:

1. Acknowledge the situation and how it happened to all relative audiences. Use facts. Avoid assigning blame to indi-

viduals since many in your audience probably approved the previous strategy. Position the current situation as "unintended consequences" and you have a plan to improve the current results.

2. Develop *your* plan to improve the situation.

3. Communicate a realistic timeline for *your* plan. You will own these results. Meanwhile, outline your current estimate of results based on what you inherited.

4. Know you will be tempted to use the Blame Game a lot until your plan works. Instead, simply remind everyone at appropriate times about your initial presentation, the facts, and your agreed-upon timeline.

5. Own the new plan. Focus on achieving your plan and results, not the past.

Now what if you are managing the blame game manager or department/division?

You instruct them to use the exact same plan as just outlined. They will most likely resist or try an end run (going to others to plead their case). Address this up front, and if it still happens, transfer or replace the lead manager. A bit harsh? No…unless you want the same poor results as the previous manager or team.

So win the game. Get rid of the blame. Get on with the new plan.

CHAPTER 65

Politics Versus Results

Many of us have learned at school, playing sports, at our job, or in life, good results matter. Let's call this group *performers*. There is another group of managers—the politicians. They appear to be accomplishing things but tend to be non-performers when it comes to results.

Now politics can derail performers and their good results quickly, even without solid business reasons, if they are not aware of their overall situation.

This theme, "politics versus results," runs through many chapters in this book. (See Chapters 1, 3, 55, 56, 60, 62, 70, 63, 66, 46.) Yes, it's a big deal.

Still, great results are the key to business growth. So how do you balance both versus getting caught between them?

Some approaches:

1. Try to include everyone in the business process (whatever it is), and recognize and reward everyone as equally as possible.
2. Spend a lot of time explaining, educating, and communicating key issues, plans, and reasons for the results and appropriate issues (politics) to all audiences.
3. Get buy-in from senior management (and/or the board, ownership if appropriate) on the plan, results, and "issue resolutions."

Here's an example.

At the consumer storage company, our division had to exit a lot of our sales, raise prices up to 25–50 percent (that's right), and accomplish this by having to work through unique sales teams of the corporation for our top three US retailers.

The other divisions and our corporate office all agreed we would exit up to $400 million of the sales in our divisions, (almost all in our division), raise prices (due to oil prices increasing plastic COGS) in all divisions, and stand together. Quickly, the politics of this agreement started brewing at all levels of our corporation, especially in all the other divisions and corporate sales (a unique top three account shared service sales team). The other divisions soon feared they would be unduly impacted by this plan (to raise prices), and the corporate sales group didn't like our move to increase prices so dramatically and our push to be more involved in the sales process. So several division presidents and the corporate sales team went back door to the CEO and the board. Everything from bonuses to who was in charge, was again presented (without us) to the CEO and board.

It was also in our customers' best interests to leverage our corporation against us. You see, they were making a lot of money (our division was losing a lot on every order) and threatened their business with other divisions against us and our very involved CEO to keep price increases and product exits down.

Politics would get everyone what they wanted here except us and the corporation's shareholders. Our results would continue to decline. Politics would win. Overall corporate results would suffer.

So we followed the three-point plan outlined earlier.

1. If we continued to lose money, the corporation's stock price would suffer. Since everyone involved here was in the stock incentive program, we used that to tie us all together (big picture).

2. We spent a lot of time reexplaining, educating, and communicating our situation to all divisions and the board/CEO. We also laid out a new plan (solution).

3. Our solution was to "take over" the top three customers sales directly. We also proposed a separate bonus program for our division with no negative impact on the other divisions. This also took away most of the customers' leverage against our other divisions. We stood alone. Made our own prices and programs, with no pricing tie-ins with our corporation's other divisions. We got senior management/ board buy-in (top corporate group sales presidents still complained but backed off—a great "Beware of what you want" moment).

We turned around a $60 million EBIT loss to $15 million gain. (See Chapters 1 and 10.) We made our special bonus program. Results beat politics. Seventy-five million dollars was restored to the corporation and its stockholders.

Business leaders, the good ones, find solutions and approve those solutions...regardless of the politics. It's a tough road but one worth traveling. It takes a committed team with a good plan and the courage to make it work.

PS Most of the divisions and corporate sales teams did not make their targets. Perhaps too much time politicizing and not enough working on results!

The CEO Blender

When you are considering joining a company or the company you are at announces a new CEO, it's important you understand who it is, where they come from, and what they have accomplished.

A CEO usually has the greatest impact on any company. Their style, strategies, track record, reputation, and background represent a very good indication of what your future can be affected by and why.

My experiences with fifteen different CEOs at ten different companies taught me many good lessons. I also learned a lot about what affects and drives CEOs. While there are plenty of great business books about successful CEOs (and not successful), there's nothing like firsthand experience.

My learnings led me to categorize CEOs into three groups:

1. Corporate experience, usually at public companies.
2. Entrepreneurs, usually with family ties.
3. Private equity, financial managers, usually who are becoming CEOs at a company their fund invested in.

Let's look into some trends I saw at each CEO group.

1. Corporate CEOs
   - The good—usually professional. They value strategic planning, employees, results, honesty, good communi-

cations, traditional organization structures, and compensation plans.

- The challenges—The CEO can be tied too closely to just what they know, also may spend too much time on stock price, buy backs, Wall Street analysts, and acquisitions. Many overpay themselves and just a select few.
- The keys—Does the CEO have a good reputation? Do people trust him/her? Has the CEO consistently had a good track record of success? Did the CEO bring in new people to his/her new companies? If all the answers are yes, that's a good sign.
- Finally, what is the CEO's record on compensation (for everyone) and stock strategy? Everyone should win here, not just the CEO. Stock buybacks are a red flag in my experience. It cuts capital spending, investment, and R&D while weakening the company. It usually rewards only the CEO group and key investors. My view here about stock buybacks (to be fair) was not popular at times with investors!
- Overall—usually a good starting place for young managers and long-term managers.

2. Entrepreneurs
- The good—You will learn a lot! This will be good and potentially not so good. Such CEOs are usually very creative, driven, cost conscious, and create new businesses, products, and services. You may also get more job opportunities than with the corporate CEO approach. You will, however, need to be successful quickly. Why? They are, so you need to be as well!
- The challenges—Entrepreneurs expect a lot since they do or have done most jobs themselves. They also find it very difficult to give up much control. This makes it difficult for you to navigate the organization and make decisions. Their polish, education, or style may also not be what you expect or even believe such a CEO should possess. Compensation and organization

structure can also be more chaotic. (Personally driven versus industry norms.) Politics, especially if family members are still in the company, will also definitely impact you (see Chapter 65). Be ready!

- The keys—This experience is invaluable if you are built for it. You will learn how to do so many more things much faster and with less resources. The risks and rewards in all areas are also higher. Yes, ask yourself the same CEO questions in the corporate list of keys, but decide, are you ready for this? Can you finish the job?

- Overall—high reward/high risk.

3. Private Equity/Many Times a First-Time Operating Company CEO

- The good—Most private equity turned CEO managers usually lack any real experience running a company, so your role can be greater than usual. This CEO type may also create more opportunities for you, including more responsibility, advancement, and higher financial rewards. Such CEOs usually push for a quicker financial exit and payouts, which could also make this a profitable situation for you. This is their background: financial management and deal making.

- The challenges—There are a lot. Such CEOs usually don't know what they don't know about running a line operation. This leads to significant issues in executing even the best of strategies. Financial "engineering" is their strong suit. This means a lot of their time is dedicated to the corporation's stock price and continuing stock buybacks. Such CEOs also focus a lot on short-term financial results. Overleveraging the company (too much debt) is also another favored approach. If this CEO's track record as a private equity manager is most or all of the aforementioned, especially if not very successful, beware. It's a tough road. It can be rewarding but also stunningly difficult and career altering.

- The keys—Like the entrepreneur CEO, you will learn a lot, both good and what not to do. The most important area to research is the private equity CEO's reputation for honesty, communications, track record, and earning trust among employees and investors.

- Overall—This CEO type is not for everyone. My experiences in every case with this type of manager, while perhaps paying you well, trust can be an issue. Sounds too harsh and a massive generalization. (I know.) It's just that it's the world they grew up in, to do what it takes to make and win the deal. It's a "who's the best buy low/sell high deal maker" contest…all the time and to the end. Knowledge is power here. If you have it and you can navigate the CEO/owners, it can work.

So if you could choose, what CEO type is best for you?

Sometimes, the new CEO could be a blend of one, two, or all three styles! The rules still apply. Whatever style is dominant under stress is the type!

So do your homework. Match your life plan (Chapter 61) to the CEO's type/track record if and when you can.

I worked for and/or with all three CEO types. For what it's worth, here are my direct experiences:

1. *Corporate CEOs.* Great trainers. Solid learnings. A resume builder and life plan foundation. Glad I didn't, however, spend my entire career in this category of CEO. Such leaders and companies can be too slow, conservative, and limiting. Politics was also a constant time waster. Still, a good leader to start with and perhaps finish.

2. *Entrepreneurs.* I learned so many things here I didn't even know I needed to know. Things like how to be so much better at speed, cost, sales, and creativity. Also, how *not* to treat people, customers, and especially suppliers. Overall, though, I admire entrepreneurs; I wish I had their moxie. I learned I was not a true entrepreneur. Their lessons, how-

ever, were invaluable. Still, as they say, if you're not family, you're not family!

3. *Private equity.* I made by far the most money with this type. I also learned absolutely the most overall here but not directly from these private equity CEOs! There were three different private equity CEOs here and one board member/investor who later became a CEO. It was very political at times, ego driven, financially dominated, and one where trust was lacking most of the time. That said, my biggest opportunities came in this environment. So it comes down to where you are, what you want, and how much you can manage. I did it. It worked despite all the issues.

    In the end, it provided me and my family with more financial freedom than I ever imagined. For that I am thankful. It's, however, a very, very challenging path. I would say it's only for the most experienced, confident, and resilient of managers!

That's the blender. Stir it up. You will get what you choose!

CHAPTER 67

Beware the Changeling

Why didn't you see it in them? Why didn't you listen? They were right there in front of you all the time. They are the changelings.

The changelings are self-focused people, and they are very challenging to successfully work with and manage. These people are experts at helping you and becoming your trusted peer or direct report. Sometimes one may even be your boss. You may know or have heard they used to be someone else's best "work" friend or peer direct report before you, but you either don't know much about it or discounted the stories. The changeling may have "changed" to you now. Everything they did before you was gone, discounted, or ignored. You may have even been told this person "turned" on other people. It just doesn't seem possible, right? Besides, this is you, and with you, the changeling is a very trusted, dependable, and good performer. You may have found or will find out; you just don't want to check out the stories about them. The changeling compliments you, helps you succeed (and you, in turn, help them succeed), and follows your lead. They protect you from potential harm and build you up to others. It's addictive. They literally "change" to be liked by you. Who doesn't like and/or want such support, (perceived loyalty) and commitment?

The problem is, it usually isn't real. The changeling is constantly evolving and waiting for the next step, and you will be the one used to get there. You may be thinking, *This won't happen to me.* You see, it probably has already happened (you just didn't know how yet), is happening, or will happen. The changeling works quietly, yes, behind your back, all the time acting as your most loyal supporter.

Still not a believer? Let's review some signs:

1. They approach you with information that will really help you (and endear them to you). It's confidential. Just between you two.
2. If and when you act on this information, you benefit. They then approach you again—can they be your friend, part of your team, or get some benefit for themselves?
3. Their previous boss or peer "warns" you and/or others about the changeling…and if you inquire about that with the changeling, they have a great response. Actually too good.
4. Others tell you how the changeling has been complimenting you to them and others.
5. The changeling then "volunteers" to help you with just about anything.

Any of these things sound or feel familiar? What to do?

1. Check out the stories.
2. Decline the special help (why hasn't the changeling told their boss or others about that secret information instead of you?).
3. Point the changeling in another direction. They will go. You will find another way to succeed.

Remember, trust is earned, not given for short-term gain. Beware the changeling as it's you they want to use.

CHAPTER 68

It Isn't True until It Happens to You

You keep hearing your coworker, boss, direct report, or perhaps someone in senior management is acting strangely, aggressive, inappropriate, or dishonestly. It, however, just doesn't seem to you that it could be true. You have not experienced any of these behaviors with the person being called out.

In fact, you may even begin to think it's the person complaining about these behaviors of the other person who is really the problem.

As a manager of the employee who is communicating these issues, it can become a larger issue. It's part of your job to listen and determine what is really going on in employee conflicts (especially if it is affecting performance of the people involved and/or the company). You may decide to ask others or go right to the source—the accused person. The problem, however, is this approach can easily backfire if (1) the accuser is not telling the truth or (2) the accused denies everything and then tries to negatively affect the accuser.

What to do?

Over time, you will find these things work themselves out. Jumping in wildly between two people too soon who can't get along usually doesn't work. If need be and they both work for you, you can get them together and encourage them to work it out. If things don't improve, then you can refer them both to HR.

Still, how do you know what is true or not? Should you ignore the whole thing? Should you go to your superior for help? The issue remains, what is true here and what can (should) you do about it?

What usually happens is most managers don't believe it or want to believe the issues are that bad. So if true, it usually gets worse.

Then it happens. Everything or part of what you have been told happens to *you*. The accused employee's behavior happens just like you've been told by the accuser. Unbelievably, you see it, regardless if you are the person's boss, coworker, or report. You are truly surprised, uncomfortable, and feeling a bit disappointed...in yourself.

You see, as one of my CEOs told me, "(Bad) behavior by other employees isn't (really) true until it happens (directly) to you."

Now you may get upset and overact. You think, why didn't you act? You also may feel you should apologize to the accuser. You can't...yet.

So now, most people go right after (if they can) the employee with problem behavior. This approach can create a bigger problem! So what's next then?

Consider the following:

1. Stop. Review what happened. Do not confront the person with poor behavior yet.
2. Get the facts.
3. Talk to others, especially HR.
4. Then talk directly to the person with poor behavior if appropriate. Get agreement on how to remedy their behavior and those affected.
5. If this is not possible, talk with HR and your superior.

In the end, the lesson here is twofold:

1. Listen better.
2. Know most things that affect you directly command most of your attention and beliefs.

So get involved right outside the personal circle of the employee with problem behavior and look for yourself...before it happens to you!

THE NEW FRONTIER

CHAPTER 69

Top of Arrowhead

Do you have a place you go to get away from everyone? Maybe to relax, work out, or just to think?

For myself, it was Arrowhead Mountain near Beaver Creek, Colorado. Only way to get to my spot was to hike there. It was about nine thousand feet high, but the trails were great, and my hike was about one thousand feet up…almost an hour up. The views were incredible. Along the way, I routinely saw deer, hawks, bears (once!), and all kinds of furry folks.

Hopefully, you have or will find your Arrowhead. It provides you with a precious gift. Solitude. Time for you. Sometimes it just lets you find that next step, whatever it is. How do you find Arrowhead?

What do you really love? Do that. Find the time often. Everyone will adjust. If really necessary, take your phone. You can make a call if need be, but try to get away for part or all of the trip.

The result? A better, happier, and more effective you.

See you at the top!

CHAPTER 70

The Penalty of (True) Leadership

The leader. Is that's who you want to be? Why? Do you believe you would be a "good leader"? Do you want power? Money? Recognition? Perhaps all these and more?

The path to leadership positions tends to be challenging. It requires acquiring useful learnings, experience, opportunities, possessing commitment, talent (usually!), drive, good financial results, and political skills.

That last point, political skills, is the double-edged sword. Leaders are involved with and impacted by the entire organization, especially those ranked above their position. Politics can help get you to key leadership positions. They can also remove you. Like discussed in Chapter 41, politics tend to be the "penalty" of true leadership. True, meaning you are an effective, respected, and trusted leader (in my book).

It's said when you are on top, everyone knows where to aim. It's also pretty clear that at no time are all audiences happy with their leader. Everyone wants something, and not everyone can be satisfied at the same time or at all.

The impact of this unhappiness, especially on an effective, results-driven, and trusted leader, is usually direct and indirect political attacks. Right here is the penalty of true leadership.

The envious, the impacted, the poor performers, the resentful, the passed-overs, and of course, certain owners all want to tear down or control the true leader for various reasons.

Being a true leader, building the company, rewarding the team, and enriching the shareholders is very difficult in its own right. To be penalized for overachieving by doing what "must be done" (as in "No good deed goes unpunished!") is common as most don't understand or don't like what is being accomplished. If you are such a leader or want to be one, prepare for this reward-penalty situation.

Be aware that most tough decisions, key strategic changes, and successes will be met with numerous emotional and political reactions.

So what can you do?

1. Stay aware of your audiences and listen well.
2. Communicate regularly to all audiences.
3. Guard against trying to dictate or to make everyone happy, but compromise where it will not negatively impact the company or plan.
4. Know some people will not ever fit into your leadership model and actions.
5. Stay focused and on plan, true to who you are and your leadership style.

Leadership is not for everyone. If it's for you, then know while penalties can slow you down, they don't have to beat you.

Turn those penalties around; send them back to those whose only commitment is to themselves. People will see this and follow.

Be true!

CHAPTER 71

Learning to Fly

"(You are) learning to fly (away), but you ain't got wings. Coming down is the hardest thing…" A famous rock star's words of wisdom.

Everyone, sooner or later, thinks about retiring.

Everyone works hard.

But when it gets to be time, like another rock singer says, "Everyone wants to go to heaven, but no one wants to die."

That kind of strikes me as what retirement can be like.

I thought the idea (I told everyone when I retired) was to do really well so you *could* retire. Enjoy what you have accomplished, spend time with your family, do what you want to do.

But you have to prepare for that. You have to think about that. You might want to have it set up before you get there!

I can remember many people saying they were going to retire in Florida, Arizona, or California—play golf, boat, do their hobbies. Your spouse, most likely, has their life pretty well set. Changing that routine will not be easy to accommodate the new you!

I had a good friend who told me, "Prepare for where you are going. Go somewhere where everyone is kind of like you." In my case, I went to the mountains and now to the beach! Where I live, nobody has a job! That's not really true—they probably have a job somewhere else, but when they are where I live, they are at their vacation home. They are boating, hiking, and are in an environment where everyone is having fun. It's what you have been working toward. It's something to think about as you plan your retirement.

He also said something else that really struck a chord: "You want to go out on top. You don't want to be that person who always is wondering why it (something you didn't like) happened to you." That's why I never believed in staying too long. We all see it: athletes and business leaders, etc., who stay too long...but when it comes to us, we think we are different (we are special), but we are not. Go out on top. Go out on your terms. Don't look back! Your real future life is *ahead* of you! Start flying!

LEARNINGS

CHAPTER 72

He's So Lucky, He Always Lands on His Feet

How many times have you heard that saying?

Yes, there are lottery winners, being "born" into wealth and being in the right place at the right time, but I would like to talk about why I believe "good" or "lucky" things don't just happen. Good things happen because you spend time gathering facts, running scenarios, preparing, but most importantly, anticipating…what can happen and what you would do about it. Think things through as if you were the other party. What will they do? We get so concerned, so tied up in our point of view, whether we are presenting a line review to a customer or presenting a major acquisition or comp program to the board, we don't anticipate the most logical answers and the next steps. Play the game options in your head…all the time. Think through *all* your possible scenarios. Anticipate these and prepare responses and then on to the next one and then the next one. Prepare for all those, and you will succeed.

A very successful WWII US general, George S. Patton, said about his famous battle with the equally successful German General Rommel, "Well, I read his damn book" (on tank warfare). Patton won the battle.

It's your career. Do you have a plan, both internally and externally? It doesn't mean you are not committed, but some things are unavoidable (like your company is sold and you are gone).

Anticipate. Be ready. Get "lucky"!

CHAPTER 73

Life Lessons

- It's impossible to commit to *maybe*.
- You can't do better than *yes*.
- Beware of what you want (for you will get it).
- Get it in writing.
- Pay the army in gold.
- Trust is a two-way street.
- Do what you say when you say.
- Take time (to stop and smell the roses).
- Tell the truth.
- Office politics are team killers.
- Make your numbers.
- Recognize and reward performance.
- Everyone is a salesman (including you).
- Learn how to write and speak well.
- Romances at work always end the same—poorly.
- Be on time.
- Race, color, sex, religion, politics, class, and family backgrounds have no place at work.
- Go in person.
- Don't tolerate bullies (it's too costly).
- Love what you do (or leave).
- Be what you want from others.
- Working for family-owned companies, for family members, is very, very difficult.

- Anticipate.
- Keep things simple.
- Embrace chaos (use it to get ahead).
- Money drives almost every decision.
- Be bold.
- There is never a good reason to swear at work.
- Keep at it. (Perseverance is 90 percent of the game.)
- Great salespeople always want to be paid on commission.
- Do better every year.
- PE firms are not your friends.
- Dress like a grown-up.
- Keep fit.
- Know your career is a long race.
- Success requires sacrifices.
- Eat well (healthy). Get enough sleep.
- All glory is fleeting.
- You will have to move sometimes.
- Listen (first).
- You most likely will be fired at least once.
- You get fired for not being good enough...or too good.
- If someone does something bad to you once, they will do it again.
- If you are at a company getting acquired, prepare to leave and stay.
- Synergies usually come in less than promised unless you are relentless.
- Be positive, it's infectious.
- Try very hard not to overreact—ever.
- When you are wrong, admit it, move on.
- When you are right, enough said!
- There are usually two sides to every story—not counting yours!
- Mentors are important.
- Everyone is replaceable.
- Pay attention, or get left behind.

BEYOND MAYBE—SOME BOOK TWO TOPICS!

- Your most important hire
- The big lie
- Viruses
- What they want to hear
- What would you do if you were them?
- Your company's real situation
- So you want to be on a board?
- How to…
- So you can work from anywhere?
- How to manage younger managers
- Why each generation is different at work
- Your home is not work

The Spouse's/Mom's Perspective on Chapter 52: But We Are Afraid of Jackie by Veronica Genito

Finding out about the potential thought of moving

This is when your spouse (husband in my case) comes home telling you that "things" are happening at the company and there "could" be changes at the office. This may last a few days to a few weeks or in some cases several months. Then one day he comes home and tells me the office is closing. All the employees are in freak-out mode as to what they should do and where to go. There is a small glimmer of hope because some people are being considered to join in this exciting move and relocate to the new office. Hurray! Then the bomb drops, and it is some God-awful place on this planet that no one with a bit of sense would want to move to unless you want to mate with a polar bear (as you may guess, this relocation ripped us out of the sunny south to the cold, barren north country.)

At this point, most people at the office are quietly and secretly sitting behind their desks, job surfing when no one is looking. Some employees get the boot, only because they didn't do anything there to begin with. A certain few are asked to come along, my husband being one of them. Soon after, there is a little weekend trip planned for those who might want to relocate or perhaps just take a sneak peek at the new area just in case there is an interest in relocating.

At this time, those few survivors get on a plane with an open mind to visit the new location, which to put another way, is the great abyss of Crap-land. (By the way, I only call it "the location" or "Crap-land" because I wouldn't want to insult anyone that unfortunately is still living there against their will and/or not against their will. That just wouldn't be very nice at all.) We get to the hotel, and there is a basket of niceties, which if you were in a tiny bit of a good mood (while perhaps thinking in your head you are moving to Hawaii) would be awesome and considered very sweet and hospitable. I, on the other hand, am in full witch mode and thinking about my youngest, we'll call her Jackie, about how she might murder us in our sleep. My other children are in college at the time. The children take the news hard, but it doesn't affect them too much because they are home only for holidays and perhaps a summer or two. Well, "Jackie" didn't quite take the news well. It was NO GO from the get go, and she was mentally thinking of which friend to live with while finishing up her high school years and emancipate from her parents at the same time. She is at this point a rising sophomore.

After many conversations about the possibility of relocating from our beautiful dream home in the "nirvana bubble town" we live in to "Crap-land," we all unanimously voted a very big negatory! So my husband, feeling good, went in the next day and told his boss, "The relocation is a No Go" because Jackie doesn't want to move.

Well, at this point, my husband is told, "You're kidding me," to "What an opportunity this is for you," blah, blah, blah and that "This would be financial suicide" and "It is time to man up to Jackie and grow some..." (well, that comment didn't actually happen)! Again, this is after several negotiations of NO, NO, NO, and more Not Going. Anyway, so as this story goes, the family did not win the "We are NOT moving" vote, because I am writing this glorious chapter.

Part II

Things get very serious, and it's now time to fly back to Crap-land and pick a home for your family in less than two weekends and hope you make the right decision because this is where you have to look at your unhappy children every day until someone potentially snaps out of it. The first day you walk through multiple houses and are thinking, *Oh no, this is hideous... I can't make it past the front door... What is the weird smell... Did they just eat fish in here... Why does this family have scary dolls in their dining room in a bassinet?* Our realtor, who has unusually large hands, is not very helpful. We ask her to see some houses on the local lake (which have been recommended to us), but she tells us "you don't want to live on the lake, that's dirty living." We finally pick out a house in haste, only because it could potentially work. At this point, you try to hold it together for "the family."

Part III

Now comes the packing up of our existing house. This is where you have to brace yourself because the relocation people come in, the realtors come in, and then last but not least the moving men come in to assess the boxes and furniture situation. At this point, if you have multiple kids, the children are calling from college with the daily dramas from "I can't do this anymore... It's too hard" to "Sorry, didn't do well on my test because I slept through the alarm" or "I got a ticket last week" or "I'm thinking of dropping this class now" all at the same time the mover is saying "Excuse me, what do I do with this?"

Now comes the meltdown of one of your kids, let's again call her "Jackie." One morning, you might see gauges in her ears! Your know, the things that enlarge your ear lobe...like that's a good idea. Another day, she decides to get baptized to another religion (not a bad one), but we are already pretty much churchgoers and already Catholic. So all this time my husband is already there at Crap-land and jet setting everywhere but where we need him most. So I decide to join in the new baptism ritual and support and watch because we are afraid...very afraid of her. In our heads, we are thinking how to make this better for her and we think how about new clothes, a car, shopping sprees? Of course, bribery works every time! But it will bite you back later, trust me. We will do everything to keep the beast quiet. It works a little bit, but we haven't gotten quite there yet. This takes some time.

Part IV

Now begins the physical moving process. The moving men start bringing everything in to the new house, more, more, more, more, only to realize some things are not going to fit because the house is NOT the same size. This was my idea because it is easier to sell a small house quickly when you are trying to get out of dodge ASAP! At this point, the movers are keeping couches, chairs, TV, wedding albums (kidding, kidding). I was beginning my meltdown. Once all the movers are gone, you can have your mental breakdown, probably on the kitchen or bathroom floor. Then you look around and one of the moving men emptied and piled fifteen to twenty boxes worth of kitchen stuff all over the floor because I agreed to have one room unpacked, and that was a very bad idea. If you touched one of the piles, you just lost the Jenga game!

Part V

So that first weekend, you might get a surprise visit from the boss, just checking to see if the WHOLE family relocated or if you said you did and really didn't because half of the family is still at the other house or hiding out with friends. Now starts the boss bribery with tickets to a show, certificates for a spa, baseball game, football game, concert, etc. It is very nice, but it only takes some of the edge off because we are still afraid of Jackie and the bomb has not detonated yet. Click, click, click. The unpacking is endless. School starts the next day, but actually we missed a few days already (my fault). This is the most difficult time to hold it all together...the drop off at school. Once you are alone in your car again, it is time to cry now all by yourself. The car will be your breakdown "go to" place.

Please, please, please, hold it together for everyone in your family and only spill it to your friends how miserable you are because even though you think this is hard for you, it is hard for your husband too—the guilt of "did I make the right move for my family?" Remember, your friends will be there for you, and you will make some new friends even if you complain to your new neighbors how this is the most awful place to live. They too will come around because you are a wonderful resilient person!

Slowly and I mean slowly, perhaps a few months but it actually starts to get better…very slowly. For those of you who might relocate for only a few months to a year or perhaps several years, you will find out later, much later, that one day your children will thank you for branching out and making it through something extremely difficult, but it won't kill you; they won't be afraid to try something new later down the road, and it will bring you closer. It will help them to not be afraid; it might help them to pursue a job in somewhere else one day.

It is tough, but the family will survive together. All of you will grow with the experience. I've done it more than once. When push comes to shove, you will be able to do it and survive. Change is constant and inevitable. It is one of the few things in life you can count on. And believe it or not, "Jackie" (the girl we call "Jackie") is very much okay.

The End.

I dedicate this chapter to Dave Lumley, the person who at one point in my life I hated more than a spider on the floor that should be stepped on, to probably having the best times of my life with him and his lovely wife. They were truly memorable times, and I want to really thank you.

All the best,
Veronica

ABOUT THE AUTHOR

Dave Lumley spent almost forty years in positions ranging from manager to CEO to BOD, boldly leading teams in developing, executing, and succeeding at nine well-known consumer companies. His passion was and still is to positively help improve company fortunes while helping build successful careers for its employees.

Built on the foundations of trust, open and direct communications, simple but very focused strategies, and relentless execution, his experiences, learnings, and consistent business and employee results provide a roadmap for managers of all levels.

As an aspiring journalist starting at fourteen years old, he discovered good oral and written communication skills were a great launching pad for business and employee success. This led to Northwestern University graduate journalism and, later, business schools. More importantly, however, were the numerous opportunities to be an important part of several business turnarounds, including sporting goods, marine, nutrition, personal care, kitchen appliances, bicycles, consumer batteries, home and garden, pet, and home consumer storage. His board roles also include major global companies in outdoor power equipment, paints, beverages, boating, and consumer goods.

His belief in the truth, open communications, and broad-based compensation are useful and enduring how-to lessons for all managers. He encourages all readers to explore their next steps—right here, right now.

Dave Lumley currently resides in California with his spouse of over thirty years. He still mentors numerous managers and consults for several boards.

CPSIA information can be obtained
at www.ICGtesting.com
Printed in the USA
LVHW040720100723
751942LV00039B/328